International Mediation

To:

Jacob Bercovitch (1946–2011)
A pioneer in the empirical study of international mediation

International Mediation

J. MICHAEL GREIG AND
PAUL F. DIEHL

polity

First published in 2012 by Polity Press

Polity Press
65 Bridge Street
Cambridge CB2 1UR, UK

Polity Press
350 Main Street
Malden, MA 02148, USA

ISBN-13: 978-0-7456-5330-3
ISBN-13: 978-0-7456-5331-0(pb)

A catalogue record for this book is available from the British Library.

Typeset in 10.25 on 13 pt Scala
by Servis Filmsetting Ltd, Stockport, Cheshire
Printed and bound in Great Britain by MPG Books Group Limited

For further information on Polity, visit our website: www.politybooks.com

Contents

Acknowledgements

The authors would like to thank David Winters and Louise Knight from Polity Press for their support and encouragement in preparing this book. We are also grateful to Ashly Townsen and Robert Diehl for their research assistance and to Jacob Bercovitch for providing most of the data used in the various analyses reported in the book.

Figures

Tables

CHAPTER ONE

Introduction

The use of mediation as a tool to manage conflicts is much older than the modern nation-state system itself. During the spring of 209 BC, a group of emissaries from several Greek city-states sought to mediate the First Macedonian War between the Aetolian League and Macedonia, producing a short truce in the conflict. This diplomatic intervention was driven not only by events on the battlefield between the belligerents, but also by the interests of the third parties themselves, each seeking to limit the expansion of Macedonian power and preserve the flow of regional commerce (Eckstein, 2002). Contemporary international mediation takes a similar form, with the diplomatic interventions of third parties into conflicts motivated by a combination of their desire to mitigate violence, establish peace, and protect their own interests. Over the last several decades, high-profile mediation efforts have played a vital role in ending decades-long civil violence in Northern Ireland, terminating the enduring rivalry between Israel and Egypt that previously experienced three major wars, and brokering the settlement of a territorial dispute between Chile and Argentina that brought those two nations to the precipice of war. In this chapter, we will discuss what mediation is, how it is used to manage conflicts in the international system, and how it differs from other conflict management approaches. We conclude the chapter with a discussion of several historic mediation efforts.

What is Mediation?

Mediation is a conflict management tool used widely across a diverse set of contentious cases, running the gamut from divorce settlement talks to labor management negotiations to peace efforts between warring states. Regardless of the type of conflict to which it is applied, the distinguishing feature of mediation is the introduction of an outside or third party into the negotiation process between the disputing sides with, at least partially, the aim of producing a settlement between the two sides. In one definition, Wall and Standifer (Wall et al., 2001: 370) define mediation simply as "assistance to two or more interacting parties by third parties who (usually) have no authority to impose an outcome." This conceptualization has the key element that mediation is voluntary on the part of disputants as well as the mediator. Yet because mediation is voluntary, it cannot be assured that every disputant will be open to attempting mediation to manage or resolve conflict. It is not uncommon, for example, for governments confronting a rebel insurgency to reject overtures for mediation. The stronger side in interstate disputes often rejects mediation of their conflicts. India, for example, has tended to resist mediation with Pakistan over Kashmir. Major power states also tend to avoid third party assistance in managing their conflicts.

Given this voluntary character, both parties in conflict must conclude that they potentially gain more by accepting mediation than they can expect to gain on their own after rejecting third-party assistance. The benefits from accepting mediation may include an end to the violence and the settlement of the conflict, but may also consist of narrower gains that are unrelated to the achievement of a diplomatic settlement. Disputants may also engage in mediation as a means of preserving their relationship with the third party offering mediation or as a way to buy time until their prospects on the battlefield improve and their ability to impose their preferred settlement on the conflict grows (Richmond, 1998). This alternative motivation is discussed in more detail in Chapter 4. Third-party mediators must be willing to devote time and resources to the effort of managing the conflict. Their motives might be altruistic, but mediators might also have a vested interest in managing a conflict or in a particular outcome. The conditions under which this occurs and which actors are most likely to serve as mediators are discussed in Chapter 3.

The simple structural definition of mediation (a third party among disputants) also emphasizes the formal role that the mediator assumes. As noted below, this can take several different forms, but in all cases the mediator is clearly a player in the conflict management process. In contrast, an actor might serve only in an advisory capacity to one side of a dispute or offer recommendations in a public forum on how the conflict might be managed. The former suggests a role in the conflict itself, but not as a mediator. The latter is not active in the direct conflict management process, even though some of the ideas might ultimately promote a settlement. Mediators have a clear and active role in the conflict management process.

Related mediation definitions emphasize less the formal role of the mediator and more decidedly the process in which the mediator alters the dynamics between the conflicting parties and their bargaining. In this respect, mediation can be described as "a mode of negotiation in which a third party helps the parties find a solution which they cannot find themselves" (Zartman, 2008: 155). Bercovitch et al. (1991: 8) describe mediation in similar terms as "a process of conflict management where disputants seek the assistance of, or accept an offer of help from, an individual, group, state, or organization to settle their conflict or resolve their differences without resorting to physical force or invoking the authority of law." Here, mediation covers a wide range of third-party activities that extend from simply providing a forum for the parties to negotiate to assisting them in formulating potential settlement terms and in which the mediator uses its influence and resources to leverage an agreement.

The primary weakness of the above definitions is that while they suggest that mediators assist the parties in settling their conflict, they lack a description of how third parties do this. Bercovitch (2002) provides some clarification in elaborating how the presence of the mediator effects change in the conflict by altering the perceptions or the behaviors of the parties. The inclusion of the changes that a mediator encourages between the parties is an important component of the definition of mediation. Because mediators can facilitate settlements between parties in conflict by offering encouragement toward agreement, persuading the reconsideration of viewpoints, offering sanctions and rewards to alter bargaining positions, and developing new ideas for potential settlement terms, the addition of a mediator to a conflict is a significant change to the dynamics of the parties' interactions.

One extension of the basic definition is to incorporate neutrality, or the political positioning of the mediator vis-à-vis the disputants. Thus, Kochan and Jick (2011: 211) see mediation as a "process in which a neutral party attempts to get the direct participants to reach a voluntary agreement." A neutral mediator is said to be one that does not favor one side or the other. This goes beyond the mediator's role as a third party who is not directly involved in the conflict, but extends to the mediator having no strong personal or national interests in how any agreement affects or favors any of the parties to the conflict or indeed the mediator itself. For many mediation efforts, such as the labor negotiations that Kochan and Jick (2011) discuss, a neutral mediator that is trusted by both sides is at the center of the mediation process. The United Nations mediation in the civil war in Tajikistan is a good example of the help that a neutral mediator can bring to the parties in conflict. The disputants were able to trust the United Nations and, in turn, the United Nations was able to improve the lines of communications between the two sides and suggest potential areas of agreement.

Despite the potential importance of neutrality in mediation, it is best that this element not be part of the central definition of mediation, but rather be considered as a potential variable in assessing the success of mediation. Indeed, not all mediation activities are carried out by individuals, groups, states, or organizations that can be regarded as neutral in a given context. For some conflicts in the international system, a neutral third party is not always available. It would be mistaken to ignore such efforts as falling outside mediation, when in fact the conflict management processes and actions are quite similar except for the identity and preferences of the mediator. It is better to assess how neutrality or lack thereof influences the likelihood of settlement, concerns that are the subject of considerable debate and which are addressed in Chapter 4. From that debate and empirical findings, it is evident that neutrality is not a necessary condition for favorable outcomes. Going into its mediation between Israel and Egypt, the United States had a clear bias toward Israel, but the combination of its role as a superpower, its interest in stability in the Middle East, and its ability to both use leverage to encourage an agreement and provide guarantees to both sides made it an attractive mediator, in spite of this bias.

Putting all these elements together and adding several others, Bercovitch and Jackson (2009: 34–35) summarize the essential characteristics of mediation:

1. Mediation is an extension and continuation of peaceful conflict resolution.
2. Mediation involves the intervention of an outsider – an individual, a group, or an organization – into a conflict between two or more states or other actors.

3. Mediation is a noncoercive, nonviolent, and, ultimately, nonbinding form of intervention.
4. Mediators enter a conflict, whether internal or international, in order to affect, change, resolve, modify, or influence it in some way. Mediators use personal or structural resources to achieve these objectives.
5. Mediators bring with them, consciously or otherwise, ideas, knowledge, resources, and interests of their own or of the group or organization they represent. Mediators often have their own assumptions and agendas about the conflict in question.
6. Mediation is a voluntary form of conflict management. The actors involved retain control over the outcome (if not always over the process) of their conflict, as well as the freedom to accept or reject mediation or mediators' proposals.
7. Mediation usually only operates on an *ad hoc* basis.

Forms of Mediation

The term "mediation" is a broad term that, in actuality, encompasses a wide range of third-party activities to manage a conflict. The approach that a third party takes in managing a conflict is dependent upon the conditions faced by the disputants. For some conflicts, the primary impediment to producing a settlement between the parties is information. In these conflicts, simply facilitating the ability of the two sides to sit down and talk may be sufficient to permit them to exchange information on their bargaining positions and goals, overcome misunderstandings, and identify areas of possible agreement. For other conflicts, how the parties see their relationship and the issues in contention are the key barriers to a settlement. In those circumstances, it is necessary for a third party to step in and help the parties to reframe their view of the conflict away from a zero-sum game toward one in which both sides come to believe that they are likely to emerge after a settlement better off than they were under the status quo. In this respect, the mediator assists the disputants in viewing their issues in contention as problems to be jointly solved. For still other conflicts, a third party is necessary to change the bargaining positions of the two sides, making settlement terms, which might initially be seen by the disputants as unacceptable, more palatable by offering rewards for their acceptance or punishments for their rejection.

One way to think about the differences in the forms that mediation takes is to focus upon the level of involvement the third party has in the conduct of the negotiations and the development of proposals to settle the conflict. Fisher (2007) distinguishes between four levels of third-party engagement: conciliation, consultation, pure mediation, and power mediation. Conciliation is the lowest level of third-party engagement; a third party focuses upon developing informal communication linkages between the disputants as a means to reduce the level of hostility between the two sides and provides the foundation for further negotiations among them. In this form of mediation, what Pruitt (2000) refers to as "light mediation," the third party is not directly involved in developing settlement solutions to the conflict or attempting to leverage concessions from the disputants. Instead, conciliation is more likely to involve a third party providing "good offices" among the disputants, simply arranging for a meeting place and time to facilitate discussions, but giving the disputants a free hand in the discussions. The Community of Sant'Egidio, a lay Catholic organization, provided such a forum for the Mozambican government and RENAMO rebels during Mozambique's civil war, allowing the two sides the opportunity to come together and lay the groundwork for the 1992 Rome General Peace Accords that ended the war.

Consultation involves a more extensive level of mediator involvement in the negotiation process itself. A mediator performing a consultative role uses personal skills and an understanding of conflict management as tools to aid disputants in moving toward a problem-solving focus in dealing with the issues under dispute. In this respect, consultation involves a more direct hand of the third party in the discussions between the two sides. This involvement, however, remains limited with the mediator avoiding efforts to exert control over the discussions, change the bargaining positions of the two sides, or offer them carrots and sticks in favor of providing encouragement to the two sides to think of the common interests that exist between the two sides in ending the conflict. During the negotiation of the Camp David Accords, President Jimmy Carter, who tended to be averse to hard bargaining, generally saw the mediation process as one in which his role was to help the Egyptian and Israeli sides reconsider the issues in dispute between them as a problem which each had a shared interest to resolve rather than one seen in zero-sum terms (Princen, 1991).

In pure mediation, the third party plays a more substantial role in the talks between the disputants, encouraging an agreement not only by attempting to reason with and persuade them, but also by controlling the information flow between the two sides and offering potential settlement terms to the conflict. In this role, the mediator becomes a solution innovator to the conflict, seeking to help the parties not only to recognize areas of common interest, but also to develop terms of settlement for the conflict, and to encourage the disputants to embrace those terms. Unlike consultation, in pure mediation the mediator exerts more extensive control over the talks. A mediator might, for example, limit the range of topics to be conducted in the negotiations in order to increase the chances for their success, excluding some issues from the talks entirely and focusing on others that seem more favorable for agreement or are better tied to the issues under contention. In mediating the Northern Ireland conflict, an ad hoc international body, headed by the US (through George Mitchell) initially limited conflict management efforts to only the "decommissioning" (disarmament) issue, with the hope that an agreement there might be a springboard to a broader settlement.

The most intensive form of mediation is power mediation. In power mediation, the mediator not only controls the issues under discussion and develops potential settlement terms to the conflict, but actively uses its resources to leverage an agreement by the parties. As such, power mediation, what Pruitt (2000) refers to as "heavy mediation" and Zartman (2008) calls "manipulation," is the most coercive form of third-party diplomatic intervention. In power mediation, the third party can use its resources as both carrots and sticks to entice the disputants toward an agreement. A third party might, for example, sweeten the terms of a potential settlement by offering foreign aid to the disputants. A third party might also push the parties toward an agreement by threatening punishments such as economic sanctions or even military strikes. In this respect, power mediation is distinct from the other three forms of mediation. Conciliation encourages agreement by improving the information flow between the sides while both consultation and pure mediation use the mediator as an additional source of ideas about potential settlement terms. Power mediation is the only form of mediation in which the third party actually changes the bargaining space over the issues between the disputants. As such, power mediation, unlike other forms, can produce a settlement to a conflict when the initial bargaining positions of the two sides have no area of overlap.

American mediation of the Camp David Accords is a good example of power mediation at work. In order to encourage agreement between Israel and Egypt, the United States offered substantial amounts of foreign aid to both Israel and Egypt while also offering security guarantees to assuage Israel's fears of Egyptian cheating. American mediator Richard Holbrooke's use of threats during the negotiation of the Dayton Accords during the Bosnian conflict is another example of the use of power mediation. Reaching an impasse in the talks over possession of the town of Brcko in northern Bosnia, Holbrooke threatened the Serbians that the talks would be declared a failure and shut down, and he suggested the potential for renewed NATO bombing of Serbian forces (Holbrooke, 1999). Serbian leader Slobodan Milosevic relented on the issue the following day and the talks continued.

Goals of Mediation

Much as mediation can take many different forms, so too can the goals of mediation efforts vary. These goals can range from the narrowest of aims, such as achieving an agreement over a tertiary issue in a conflict, to a full settlement of all the issues in dispute. A third party might, for example, mediate an agreement on prisoner exchanges between two warring states. Achievement of such an agreement positively addresses the prisoner issue between the two sides, yet leaves the fundamental issues in dispute that caused the war unresolved.

A cease-fire is one way in which mediation can assist in successfully managing a conflict. By brokering a cease-fire, a mediator can not only stop the death and destruction caused by the conflict at least temporarily, but can also buy time to reduce the level of hostility between the two sides. In this respect, while a cease-fire does not necessarily end a conflict, it can create a lull in the fighting that is sufficient for the two sides to reconsider their options and potentially transition toward more peaceful means of settling their dispute.

Although achieving a cease-fire is often beneficial, the degree to which it improves the relationship between warring parties can vary significantly. In some conflicts, cease-fires break down quickly. As a result, producing a cease-fire that collapses within days, or even hours, is not always a significant contribution to peace. Along these same lines, achievement of a cease-fire does not always indicate momentum toward a broader peace. Warring parties can sometimes sign on for a cease-fire because they see it as a means to gain breathing space that will improve their ability to achieve their goals on the battlefield or exert more leverage over the other side during negotiations (Princen, 1992; Richmond, 1998).

Although a cease-fire can halt, at least temporarily, the violence between warring parties, it leaves the underlying issues in dispute unresolved. In order to achieve a comprehensive peace that is likely to be durable, the parties must not only stop fighting but must also settle their differences that caused the conflict in the first place. Otherwise, there remains a continued risk of flare-ups between the contending sides as each tries to impose a settlement on the disputed issues. For many conflicts, violence is caused by disagreements over a broad range of issues of varying complexity. Under these circumstances, it can be undesirable, if not impossible, to attempt to resolve all of the issues in dispute at once. Instead, a mediator may choose to focus discussions on a particular subset of issues for which agreement is likely to be the easiest or on which tensions between the parties are the lowest in order to facilitate progress in the talks. Under these circumstances, a mediator will pursue the achievement of a series of partial agreements over time, often on procedural or less controversial issues, as a means to build toward a broader settlement of the conflict.

The International Negotiation Network intervened in the conflict between Ethiopia and Eritrea in September 1989 with the first simple goal of reaching an agreement on the meeting's agenda. Subsequently, they reached agreements on rules for subsequent meetings including all of the following: publicity, languages, official records, venue, procedural rules, time/place of next meeting, agenda, and rules for delegations. Sixty days later, they met in Nairobi for the main talks. These talks included agreements on power-sharing between the leadership from both sides and on some territorial and political divisions. The organization specifically designed the first meetings to force the combatants to agree on minor procedural matters before moving on to more difficult issues.

Partial agreements can contribute to the development of a broader peace between the two sides. Partial agreements, by producing settlements of some issues and removing them from the agenda of issues in dispute between the parties, often make future agreements easier by reducing the complexity of those future talks (Bercovitch and Langley, 1993; Greig and Diehl, 2005; Hopmann, 1996). By providing a basis for disputants to build trust with one another, partial agreements can also create an environment where the disputants use agreements over more minor issues to build momentum toward the settlement of the key issues under dispute (Greig, 2001; 2005; Regan and Stam, 2000; Zubek et al., 1992). The risk, however, is that reducing the number of issues in bargaining can prevent the kind of trade-offs across those issues that might be necessary for a comprehensive settlement (Brams and Taylor, 1996).

Achievement of a full settlement is the most ambitious goal of a mediation effort. In doing so, a full settlement lays the foundation for a sustainable peace between the two sides. Those conflicts in which both settlement and agreement implementation are easiest are unlikely to call for the assistance of a mediator in the first place because the parties are able to negotiate a settlement bilaterally. Those conflicts that do require the assistance of a mediator tend to be the most resistant to settlement and durable peace. In this respect, mediated conflicts, because of the way in which they select themselves for mediation, are at especially high risk of achieving settlements that prove to be short-lived (Gartner and Bercovitch, 2006).

The danger of short-lived agreements points to the important distinction between mediation goals and mediation success. One way to think about the success of mediation is by focusing upon the goals of the mediation effort itself. As Kleiboer (1996) argues, gauging mediation success in terms of the goals of the mediation makes it difficult to identify mediation success consistently. It is not always easy to identify the initial goals of the parties that participate in a mediation effort, nor is it always the case that these goals remain constant during the peace process. Even if we can clearly identify these goals, should it be the goals of the mediator or the disputants that matter in determining the success or failure of mediation? What if the goals of the mediator and the disputants are different from one another? In the Suez Crisis, the United States as third party sought international control of the waterway whereas the disputants (Egypt, Israel, UK, and France) sought control themselves or full open access. For these reasons, scholars of mediation often focus upon more objective indicators of its success. Among these objective indicators, there is a clear dichotomy between those that have short-term effects and those that have a long-term impact on a conflict (Beardsley, 2008; Gartner and Bercovitch, 2006; Greig, 2001). For example, former US President Jimmy Carter helped defuse a nuclear crisis with North Korea in 1994, but that success proved short-lived as the nuclear proliferation and other tensions in that region would repeatedly resurface within the next decade.

A large segment of the scholarly literature (Bercovitch and

Gartner, 2006; Bercovitch and Langley, 1993; Svensson, 2007b; Wilkenfeld, et al., 2003) focuses on agreements as the most important indicator of short-term mediation success. The appeal of an agreement as an indicator of short-term success is obvious. Mediated agreements are nearly always prominently reported, making them readily observable. At the same time, a mediated agreement is an objectively observable indicator of progress in the relations between conflict sides (Diehl and Druckman, 2010). Because mediated agreements may not be durable and may not effect changes in the actions of the parties in conflict, other scholars focus on changes in the behavior of the parties during a conflict as an indicator of successful mediation. Some (Dixon, 1996; Rauchhaus, 2006) emphasize the impact of mediation on limiting conflict escalation while others (Regan and Aydin, 2006; Regan and Stam, 2000; Wilkenfeld et al., 2003) envision mediation success in terms of its ability to lessen the duration of an individual, ongoing military conflict. Quinn et al. (2006), for example, focus upon the ability of mediation to reduce tensions between states involved in a crisis.

The second approach to identifying mediation success focuses on the long-term effects of mediation beyond its effects in a single conflict. The logic here is that mediation in its most successful outcomes changes the dynamics of the relationships between the disputants, making them less prone to use violence against one another in the future and more likely to resolve their disputes peacefully. Beardsley (2006) conceptualizes mediation success as an increase in the length of time between crises for a pair of states. In a similar vein, Greig (2001) operationalizes mediation success by looking at the duration between a mediation effort and the next militarized dispute between rival states. Even if violent conflict cannot be prevented, mediation might at least delay its onset. A key weakness of these approaches is that they make it difficult to draw a sharp line between cases of mediation success and mediation failure. Instead, these long-term conceptualizations of mediation success are better suited to thinking of mediation success along a continuum from less successful to more successful.

In the end, just as there is no one-size-fits-all choice for the ways in which third parties mediate conflicts, the same holds true for the goals of an individual mediation effort and the way in which its success or failure is determined. Instead, third parties choose the goals of an individual mediation effort by taking into consideration the characteristics of the disputants, the history of prior conflict management efforts applied to the dispute, and the characteristics of the conflict. In this same way, analysts of mediation must adjust their measures of mediation success to fit the conflicts that they seek to understand and explain. What mediation success means varies from context to context (Bercovitch, 2002).

Mediation according to Stages and Phases of Conflict

The discussion above implies that mediation exists regardless of conflict context and assumes intervention into an ongoing process of bargaining between the disputants. In fact, mediation might occur during several phases of the conflict process and take place before, during, and after outbreaks of violence. Accordingly, the goals and forms of mediation, and their relationship to other conflict management techniques discussed below, might be different.

Roughly, there are four different "phases" of conflict in which mediation might occur: pre-violence, during armed conflict, after a cease-fire, and following a peace agreement (Diehl, 2006). Not all conflicts go through each of these phases, and the process is not unidirectional – that is, a conflict can move from one phase (armed conflict or cease-fire respectively) backward (no violence or armed conflict respectively) as well as forward. Similarly, there are three different "stages" that might be described in terms of the conflict resolution process: "getting to the table," getting to an agreement, and implementing the agreement respectively (Walter, 2002). Conflict phases and resolution stages intersect and influence the process and strategies of mediation.

Mediation deployment in the pre-armed conflict phase involves a third party participating in conflict management because of the future risk of violence escalation rather than ongoing armed conflict. In this phase, it might be difficult to get parties to the table unless the threat of military action is high, but if the disputants have experienced several wars in the past, they might be more willing to negotiate and perhaps ultimately come to an agreement. Nevertheless, the United Nations provided good offices and attempted mediation in the months leading up to the Argentine invasion of the Falkland/ Malvinas Islands, but no agreement was reached. There are some advantages to mediation at this stage. If mediation can forestall armed attacks, widespread killing, waves of refugees, and dislocations of the economy, there are clearly benefits to all. At the macro-level, preventing violent conflict may make it easier to promote conflict resolution in the long run, as the increased hatred and mistrust from any war are avoided and the consequences of the armed conflict do not have to be factored into potential settlements.

Intervention during the second conflict phase, while military hostilities are ongoing, modifies the goals for mediation. A cease-fire is most often the immediate goal and longer-term concerns are typically deferred until that has occurred. Just getting the combatants to the table is an important step, but any agreement is likely to be limited. Nevertheless, mediation at this phase of the conflict might be necessary in order to advance the conflict into another phase. Cease-fires were agreed to at multiple junctures of the Bosnia civil war, but many of these broke down before any broader settlement was negotiated. Nevertheless, a ccase-fire was negotiated among combatants just prior to the achievement of the Dayton Accords, ending the conflict.

A third phase occurs following a cease-fire, but prior to res-olution of the underlying disputes between the hostile parties. One might presume that mediators have already secured deci-sions by the parties involved at least to halt hostilities, but this does not necessarily mean the disputants are ready to come to the table to negotiate terms of settlement. Thus, a cease-fire might mean that mediators must return to the first stage, even as violence is temporarily halted by a successful diplomatic intervention. Various European Union mediation efforts have attempted to craft a final peace settlement in Cyprus as a long-standing cease-fire monitored by United Nations peace-keeping forces insured that the conflict would not revert back to an earlier conflict phase.

The final phase of conflict occurs after a peace settlement is achieved. Yet this does not mean that the mediator's job is over, only that the conflict resolution process has entered its third juncture. Although disputants have agreed to terms of a full or partial settlement, there are a variety of concerns and disagreements that will arise over how those terms are imple-mented and in some cases whether the parties have actually kept their parts of the bargain. Mediators then become con-cerned with many short-term measures and issues that might undermine the settlement agreement; the clear risk is that the agreement will unravel and the conflict will revert back to phase 2. For example, the United Nations served as a mediator between the combatants following the 1992 peace agreement that ended El Salvador's civil war and through the 1994 elections to prevent the recurrence of conflict.

Thus, mediation is not unique to a certain phase of conflict, but occurs within many different contexts. Mediation is also not confined to the stage of conflict resolution whose results are most visible, namely when enemies reach a peace agreement. Mediation might be necessary to get those parties bargaining with one another, and might be equally important in facilitating the implementation of an agreement that prevents a return to hostility and armed conflict.

Mediation versus Other Conflict Management Approaches

Mediation is not the only conflict management approach available to actors, but it is sometimes confused with related strategies. Most notably, negotiation and mediation are often used interchangeably. Indeed, they share several procedural elements, including bargaining in formal and semi-formal settings involving key participants in conflict. Yet mediation differs from negotiation in several ways. Clearly, the addition of a third party actor to the bargaining undertaken by the primary conflict actors represents a structural change; this is not merely the addition of another participant, but a qualitatively different approach in that the mediator is not a direct participant in the ongoing dispute. Equally important, as noted above, mediation changes the dynamics of bargaining between the conflict parties, and thus the processes and outcomes of the conflict management attempt are likely to be quite different. In this respect, mediation is best seen not as a special form of negotiation, but as a distinct form of conflict management (Dixon, 1996).

Mediation is not synonymous with other conflict management approaches such as fact-finding (inquiry) or "good offices," even as it might encompass them in some fashion during the mediation process. Fact-finding is predicated on providing information necessary for the disputants to resolve their conflict. This is not an essential element of mediation, but mediators often serve as formal and informal conduits for information collection and transmission. "Good offices" is only the achievement of bringing the disputing parties together, but includes no role for the third party in the process of bargaining such as recommending solutions or participating in discussions. As referenced above, light mediation can involve this conflict management approach, but it is not limited to this kind of role; mediation frequently comprises a more active role in the conflict management process.

Mediation often involves putting forth recommendations for settlement to the disputants, but this is different from other processes that also offer solutions to the dispute, such as conciliation, arbitration, and adjudication. Similar to some mediation attempts, conciliation involves a third party that offers a recommended solution to the parties involved, who retain control over the outcome by being able to accept or reject that recommendation. Yet the third party acts more as a hearing officer, listening to the facts presented by each side, rather than being part of a bargaining process itself, which is characteristic of a mediator. Thus, a conciliator maintains some distance from the conflicting parties and attempts to craft a solution based on fairness. A mediator is active in the process and might make several suggestions for resolution (or none at all), and these might be based as much on terms that are most likely to be accepted by the parties as on abstract notions of equity.

Arbitration more closely resembles conciliation except that the former includes the third party actually deciding the outcome, as the decision of the arbitrator is binding on the disputants according to prior agreement. In contrast, one of the defining features of mediation is that the parties, not the mediator, retain control over the outcome. Similarly, adjudication is several more steps removed from mediation, in that binding decisions are rendered in formal proceedings with defined rules and confined to disputes that can be resolved by reference to legal standards. The forms and processes of mediation are not so restricted nor is mediation limited to legal concerns; legal rules might be useful to mediators (e.g. drawing an international boundary), but the conflict resolution is not dependent on them nor is the purview of mediation limited to legally based disputes.

Many other approaches to peace and conflict management bear little similarity to mediation, although their application is not necessarily mutually exclusive of mediation efforts. Peacekeeping is also a third-party intervention into conflict, but it is a field exercise, directly addressing the manifestations of the dispute on the ground. Soldiers, not diplomats, assume the third-party role. Although one of the purposes of peacekeeping might be to facilitate a settlement between parties (Diehl and Druckman, 2010), it aspires to do so indirectly by providing a proper environment for such a peaceful settlement rather than being a part of deliberations. Other conflict management approaches, such as the imposition of economic sanctions and military intervention, are coercive in character and involve direct punishment of conflict parties. Their purposes are generally not to stimulate negotiations, but rather to alter the conflict behaviors of those involved. These actions are quite different from the kinds of carrots and sticks that mediators might use to induce parties to come to the bargaining table or accept a settlement.

Oslo Accords

The Oslo Accords between Israel and the Palestine Liberation Organization (PLO) are an example of mediation in which the third party employs little leverage against the disputants in the bargaining process. Instead, the key contribution of the Norwegian mediation team was in facilitating communications between the Israeli and Palestinian sides. This was done both through Track II diplomacy in which talks were conducted between Israeli academics and representatives of the PLO. These talks were subsequently followed by Track I talks between both Israeli and PLO officials. Although the Norwegian mediation effort was able to improve communications between the two sides and successfully produce an agreement between them, the difficulty of implementing the agreement produced by the Oslo peace process highlights some of the drawbacks to light mediation.

During the 1990s, global political shifts saw both Israel and the PLO facing an altered strategic environment that made them more amenable toward dialogue with one another. For the PLO, the end of the Cold War dried up Soviet financial resources for the organization and PLO support of Iraq during the Gulf War sharply undermined its support among the Arab Gulf states (Bercovitch, 1997; Kelman, 1997; Pruitt, 1997). At the same time, Israel found itself bearing the costs of containing the Palestinian intifada while both sides felt pressure by the increasing influence of Hamas (Pruitt et al., 1997). Put together, these forces contributed to the development of a situation in which the status quo was too painful to continue for the two sides (Pruitt, 1997). These conditions, coupled with Israel's prior history of negotiations with its Arab neighbors at the Madrid Conference in 1991 and Egypt at Camp David, should have created both the motivation for negotiations between Israel and the PLO and a basis for optimism for their success. Yet, the state of the relationship between Israel and the PLO posed a significant roadblock toward any diplomacy between the two sides. Prior to Oslo, the PLO refused to recognize Israel's right to exist and had no formal linkages with the Israeli government. Israel, in turn, refused dialogue with the PLO. Until 1993, it was, in fact, illegal for Israelis to have contact with PLO officials.

The state of relations between Israel and the PLO provided an opportunity for a neutral third party to facilitate talks between the two sides. Establishing these talks, however, was a delicate matter. Because of the tense relations between the two sides, it was vital that any talks among them be conducted in secret. Leaks of any potential agreement between Israel and the PLO would not only change the emergence of spoilers aimed at derailing the agreement, but publicly revealing any contact between Israel and the PLO ran the risk of collapsing the talks. The Israeli government feared the political consequences both at home and in the region of engaging in formal talks with the PLO, particularly if the PLO was not serious about producing an agreement. At the same time, the PLO, already weakened by the loss of substantial external financial support and the increasing power of Hamas, feared that talks with a potentially intransigent Israeli side would further weaken the organization. The assistance of a third party capable of improving communications between the two sides while recognizing the need for both secrecy and discretion was vital to the agreement that eventually emerged from Oslo. The Norwegian mediation team was well suited to this role.

The opening dialogue between Israel and the PLO was begun through a Norwegian research foundation, the Institute for Applied Social Sciences (FAFO). Officials at FAFO had built relationships with members of the Palestinian community, including individuals within the PLO leadership, while engaged in a project sponsored by the Norwegian government studying conditions within the West Bank and Gaza Strip. In 1992, Yossi Beilin, Deputy Foreign Minister in Israel's newly elected Labor government, met with Terje Larson, the head of FAFO, in an effort to stimulate talks between Israel and the PLO. A key condition, however, was that Israeli officials would not meet with members of the PLO. Instead, talks were arranged between two Israeli academics with ties to the Israeli government and members of the PLO. All total, there were twelve rounds of secret meetings in Norway between the Israeli academics and the PLO between January and August 1993.

During the first few rounds of talks, the Israeli scholars and PLO representatives made progress in producing a draft of principles between the sides that framed the discussions. Progress was sufficiently substantive that after the fifth meeting between the two sides Israel responded to PLO representative Abu Ala's request for an official representative to join the talks by dispatching Uri Savir, Director General of the Israeli Foreign Ministry (Pruitt et al., 1997). Savir was subsequently joined in the talks by an advisor to the Israeli Foreign Ministry. With the addition of official Israeli representatives, the secrecy of the talks became all the more imperative as each side feared the political repercussions at home of negotiating with the other side. That said, the secrecy of the talks did afford some important benefits. Keeping the parties isolated and outside the glare of the media while holding the negotiation teams small kept the talks informal, limited grandstanding, and encouraged the development of a personal understanding between the negotiators that facilitated agreement (Bercovitch, 1997; Bien, 2000; Pruitt, 1997). Conducting the negotiations in secret did have an important drawback: it prevented the negotiators from preparing the public and other elites for the agreement that was ultimately reached (Kelman, 1997). This became problematic as key sources of opposition to the agreement emerged after its drafting, both within the Israeli Knesset and the PLO hierarchy.

Members of the Norwegian mediation team largely played the role of "active facilitators" in the talks in that they focused their efforts on providing a forum and stimulating communications between the two sides to help Israeli and PLO representatives find their own solution to the conflict (Bien, 2000). During the majority of the talks, the Norwegians were largely non-intrusive, generally leaving the Israeli and PLO representatives to their own devices in the conduct of the negotiations (Pruit et al., 1997). The Norwegians did involve themselves more directly in the negotiations when it was seen as necessary to keep the talks on track. During the final round of talks, PLO leader Yasser Arafat pulled back from a key concession made in the negotiations by his representatives, threatening to derail the talks (Pruitt et al., 1997). In response, the Norwegian mediation team traveled to Stockholm to meet secretly with Israeli Foreign Minister Shimon Peres. During this visit, Norwegian Foreign Minister Johan Holst conducted phone negotiations with Yasser Arafat, relaying information between the Israeli and Palestinian sides during an eight-hour period.

This intervention salvaged the peace process and produced an accord that was formally signed by Israel and the PLO in Washington on September 13, 1993. The Oslo Accords granted mutual recognition to both Israel and the PLO, called for Palestinian self-governance in the West Bank and Gaza, and placed on the agenda negotiations to address border and settlement issues, including the final status of Jerusalem. Although the Oslo Accords show the impact that a mediation process backed by a neutral third party with few power resources can have in producing an agreement between two sides with a long history of conflict, the aftermath of the accords also shows the limitations of this form of mediation. Because the peace process depended so much upon the motivation of the two sides to make peace in order to achieve an agreement, implementation of the agreement also required substantial motivation by both sides because it lacked any enforcement mechanism or third party guarantee. As this motivation began to wane when opposition to the agreement emerged among both Israelis and Palestinians, implementation of the Oslo Accords became threatened. Ultimately, with the outbreak of the Second Intifada, the momentum toward peace created at Oslo was effectively destroyed.

Beagle Channel Dispute

Although the Oslo Accords are an example of the way in which a neutral third party with few power resources and little leverage over the disputants can facilitate a mediated agreement, the Vatican mediation of the Beagle Channel Dispute shows the influence that a third party with few power resources but an important linkage to both sides can have in mediating a conflict. The Beagle Channel Dispute centered on competing claims by Chile and Argentina over three islands south of Tierra Del Fuego and the accompanying waters surrounding them.

The dispute was a consequence of the treaty that initially set the boundaries of the two countries at their independence. The Boundary Treaty of 1881 gave Chile possession of the islands south of the Beagle Channel without specifying where precisely the Beagle Channel actually terminated (Laudy, 2000). While possession of the islands remained in contention between Chile and Argentina, interest in the resources of the territorial waters grew over time, heightening their perceived strategic importance to both sides. In an effort to resolve the dispute, both countries agreed to submit the dispute to arbitration by Great Britain in 1971. During the arbitration process, both sides submitted arguments for their positions to a five-judge panel. This panel, in turn, issued a ruling that Britain could either recommend acceptance or rejection of the ruling by Chile and Argentina. In May 1977, the panel issued a decision awarding the three disputed islands to Chile and requiring implementation of the ruling within nine months. Britain recommended acceptance of this ruling. Argentina, however, still maintained its claims to the territories; talks with Chile aimed at working out details of implementing the ruling were used by Argentina as a means, instead, to continue to press its case and negotiate over possession of the islands.

By 1978, Argentina had formally rejected the arbitration ruling and relations between the two sides deteriorated sharply. On December 12, 1978, the foreign ministers of Chile and Argentina met in Buenos Aires and quickly agreed to request mediation from the Pope. That same day, the agreement to call for Vatican intervention collapsed as Argentina's military junta stripped the Argentine president of the authority to request the mediation effort. During this time, Argentina had begun planning for war with Chile, drawing up plans for Operation Soberania in which Argentina would invade Chile and occupy the islands around Cape Horn. Thereafter, the military plan called for Argentina to continue hostilities depending upon Chile's response to the invasion. Although the invasion was planned for December 22, 1978, weather in the region caused Argentina to delay the attack by a day. At this point, recognizing the urgency of the situation, Pope John Paul II dispatched Cardinal Antonio Samoré on December 23 to the two countries as his personal envoy to the conflict.

Samoré conducted the mediation in three stages. The first stage consisted of shuttle diplomacy between the two capitals in order to dial down tensions between the two sides during December and January 1978. During this shuttle diplomacy, Samoré spent roughly equal time in both capitals, focusing his efforts on gathering information and transmitting proposals between the two sides (Laudy, 2000). The choice of shuttle diplomacy over another form of mediation was consistent with the status of the conflict that the Vatican faced.

Because Argentina and Chile had come so close to war with one another, the level of hostility between the two sides was high, making face-to-face negotiations difficult. The challenges of face-to-face negotiations were all the more apparent because of the frequency with which the two sides had, with few positive results, previously negotiated directly with one another in the dispute. Using shuttle diplomacy between the two sides allowed Samoré to lessen the emotional aspect of the negotiations while improving his ability to build trust between the two sides and gather the information from them that would be necessary for moving them toward an eventual settlement. The Vatican made sure to spend an equivalent amount of time with each side, underscoring the importance that they attached to an appearance of neutrality between the two sides. The shuttle diplomacy culminated with Chile and Argentina signing the Act of Montevideo on January 8, 1979, in which they established a framework for papal mediation of the conflict.

The second stage of the mediation process transitioned away from shuttle diplomacy to talks with the two parties in Rome conducted by Samoré as the Pope's formal representative. These talks began in May 1979. During this time, each side presented its case to the Vatican separately with virtually no direct talks held between Chile and Argentina. This process allowed the Vatican to develop a clearer picture of the positions of the two sides and the bargaining distances between them. Although Samoré applied no specific pressure for concessions on the two sides during this time, he did exert substantial control over the process. Both sides were told that their proposals would be edited to exclude any potentially inflammatory language before being delivered to the other side; all negotiations were to be conducted in secret, no concessions were final until a permanent agreement was signed, and some topics were to be excluded from the discussion

(Laudy, 2000). Conducting the mediation in this manner afforded several benefits. First, placing the parties in a controlled environment in which secrecy could be maintained limited the potentially negative influence of outside actors on the peace process. Second, bringing the parties to Rome but keeping them separated allowed the Vatican the benefit of gathering information from both sides quickly and easily while also controlling the flow between them. Keeping the sides separated allowed Samoré to avoid the possibility of emotions running high and harsh words being exchanged if the parties negotiated face to face, something that might collapse the peace process entirely.

Nevertheless, separating the parties did come with a cost. Given the high level of hostility between the two sides and the low level of trust each had for the other, maintaining a separation of the two diplomatic teams did little to improve relations between them. One of the benefits of removing disputants to an isolated location is to create an environment in which, despite all of their disagreements, each finds itself in the same boat as the other and develops a sense of camaraderie that facilitates an agreement. This logic inspired the format and location of the talks that produced the Dayton Accords during the Bosnian conflict and the Camp David Accords between Israel and Egypt. Maintaining the separation of the delegations from Chile and Argentina, while it avoided the risks of blow-up derailing the talks, also limited the ability of the two sides to develop a rapport with one another that might foster a problem-solving approach to the negotiations.

The process of each side providing information regarding its positions and views over the myriad of issues in dispute continued through the remainder of 1979 and into 1980 with little progress made across any of the issue areas. By September 1980, Samoré concluded that there was still no hope for agreement by the two sides on a comprehensive settlement of the conflict. As a result, the Pope decided to issue his own proposal for the settlement of the conflict. The Pope offered this proposal in December 1980, awarding Chile all of the disputed islands but granting Argentina navigation rights in the area waters and establishing an area of shared resource rights for both countries in a part of the Pacific Ocean that the Pope named the Sea of Peace. Chile accepted the Pope's proposal while Argentina never officially responded to it, apart from expressing significant concerns over its details.

After this period, negotiations continued between the two sides following the same basic framework of each side presenting its proposals to Samoré for the next several years with only limited progress occurring during this period of time. The major break in the dispute took place in December 1983 when military rule ended in Argentina and a new democratic government was elected. This government placed a high priority on settling the dispute with Chile. As a result, Chile and Argentina engaged in series of direct talks that led to a declaration of peace and friendship between the two sides and a request for renewed Vatican mediation to solve the Beagle Channel issue. The Vatican obliged, requesting settlement proposals from both sides. Based on these proposals the Vatican issued a new plan to settle the conflict. Both Chile and Argentina agreed to the Vatican proposal and, ultimately, signed the Treaty of Peace and Friendship in November 1984, formally resolving the Beagle Channel dispute. The Islands were awarded to Chile, but Argentina retained maritime passage rights in the entire Beagle Channel. The parties also created a Conciliation Commission and Arbitral Tribunal to deal with any future disputes.

CHAPTER TWO

The Application of Mediation to Violent Conflicts

The international system has seen marked changes in violent conflict during the post-World War II period. Conflicts have increasingly been concentrated within states, rather than between them, and the locus of conflict has shifted away from the Western Hemisphere and Europe toward Africa and Asia (see Harbom and Wallensteen, 2010; Sarkees and Wayman, 2010). Not surprisingly, these shifts have brought with them changes in the application of international mediation. After 1945, mediation has become a frequently used conflict management tool, particularly following the end of the Cold War, which is conventionally designated as 1991. This increased application of mediation, while consistent with the expansion of conflict in the international system, is only loosely tied to *where* most conflicts occur. In the following sections, we will explore how the usage of mediation has changed and the geographic areas where it is most commonly applied, and will compare these changes to the evolution of conflict in the international system. We will also examine why some conflicts seem especially resistant to mediation.

Identifying Instances of Mediation

In order to track the use of mediation in conflicts, we first need to identify all the instances in which mediation occurred in the context of armed conflicts. To do so, we turn to the best and most complete collection of data on international conflict management: Bercovitch's (2004) International Conflict Management Dataset. This data set defines mediation attempts operationally as those efforts in which a third party "facilitates communication processes in the negotiation process and may offer proposals to the parties to help them move towards agreement" (Bercovitch, 2004: 188). Included under the heading of mediation are third-party efforts at conciliation, good offices, and inquiry/fact-finding. The data examine the application of conflict management efforts to a broad array of conflicts, both interstate and civil, in the international system. Here, conflict is defined broadly, including organized military conflict as well as incidences in which there is a "demonstration of an intention to use military force" that involve at least one state (Bercovitch, 2004: 1). In this respect, the data encompass mediation efforts for conflicts including both hot wars such as the Six Day War and the Nicaraguan Contra War and conflicts on the brink of war such as the Berlin Crisis and the Beagle Channel Crisis respectively.

This collection begins in the immediate post-World War II era (1945) and extends through 1999. Although we would like to have data that include the twenty-first century, we nonetheless have more than fifty years of data on which to detect patterns, including almost a decade following the end of the Cold War. In the period studied, there have been 2,632 individual mediation efforts attempted, spread across 333 different conflicts – both civil and interstate. Because conflict is defined broadly in the data, we separate out specific types of conflicts for attention. We use data from the Correlates of War (COW) project, the largest systematic data-gathering project on conflict in the international system, to identify interstate wars, militarized interstate disputes, and civil wars.

Data on interstate wars come from the COW Interstate War Dataset 4.0 (Sarkees and Wayman, 2010), which defines wars as conflicts involving sustained violence between the armed forces of two or more states that produce at least 1,000 battle deaths in a year. Militarized interstate disputes (MIDs) are "cases of conflict in which the threat, display or use of military force short of war by one member state is explicitly directed towards the government, official representatives, official forces, property, or territory of another state" (Jones et al., 1996). In this respect, MIDs are militarized events that fall short of war. Both the Cuban Missile Crisis and the 2010 North Korean sinking of the South Korean warship *Cheonan* are examples of MIDs. We employ data from the COW Militarized Interstate Dispute Dataset 3.1 (Ghosn et al., 2004) to identify cases of MIDs. Finally, we use data from the COW Intra-State War Dataset (Sarkees and Wayman, 2010) to identify cases of civil war. A civil war is defined as a conflict involving a government against a non-state actor, the government of a regional subunit against a non-state actor, or conflict between two or more non-state actors within a state involving at least 1,000 battle-deaths over a twelve-month period.

Change in the Use of Mediation across Time

If mediation were wholly independent of conflict demand, we would expect a random pattern of mediation attempts over time or at least one that is not correlated with the incidence of violent conflict in the world. In contrast, were mediation responsive solely to demand, then mediation attempts should parallel ebbs and flows in conflict frequency. As it turns out, neither extreme is reflected in the data, although there is some merit to the latter especially in the immediate post-World War II decades. Figure 2.1 describes the frequency of mediation by decade during this period.

Of the 2,632 total mediations that took place over this 55-year period, nearly 64% occurred during the 1990s. This represents a dramatic increase from the relatively infrequent

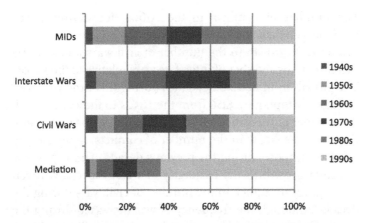

Figure 2.1 Total Share of Conflicts and Mediation by Decade

use of mediation during the 1940s and 1950s, periods that, respectively, account for 2.2% and 3.3% of total mediations between 1945 and 1999. The use of mediation to deal with conflicts in the international system began to rise significantly during the 1960s, more than doubling from 1950-levels. Mediation increased by another third during the 1970s, with its use leveling off during the 1980s.

To some extent, the initial changes in the frequency of mediation follow a trajectory similar to changes in the frequency of conflict across time. This suggests that conflict demand (how many ongoing conflicts are available for mediation) is an important determinant of mediation frequency, but there are some notable deviations in this relationship. Figure 2.1 includes data on the frequency of two types of war (civil and interstate) as well as on militarized interstate disputes short of war, as many mediation efforts are applied at lower stages of conflict in an effort to prevent escalation. Roughly coterminous with mediation attempts, the number of conflicts per decade increased from the 1950s through the 1970s.

The number of conflicts in the 1960s, for example, was 57.1% larger than the number during the 1950s. The 1960s saw a 73.3% growth in the number of civil wars and a 16.7% increase in the number of interstate wars relative to the 1950s. The growth in militarized disputes during this time was even stronger, jumping by 34% from the 1950s to the 1960s. Still, the number of mediation efforts during the 1960s grew more than twice as fast than the number of conflicts, increasing by 138% from those during the previous decade. The 1970s saw a further growth in the frequency of wars, especially driven by a significant uptick in the number of civil wars during the decade. Although the frequency of war increased during the 1970s, the amount of lower-level interstate conflict declined, with the number of militarized disputes during this decade actually dropping by 17%. The number of conflicts and mediation efforts during the 1970s grew at a roughly similar pace, with the frequency of conflicts increasing by 67% and the number of mediations growing by 58%. The 1970s saw a number of high-profile mediation efforts directed at some of the most dangerous and intractable conflicts. Among these were US Secretary of State Kissinger's mediation of the 1973 Yom Kippur War and American President Carter's mediation, resulting in the Camp David Accords between Egypt and Israel. Not only did these two mediation efforts limit violence between the two sides and stabilize their relations, but the Yom Kippur talks provided the foundation for the Camp David peace process. We will further explore the linkages across mediation efforts in subsequent chapters.

The increase in conflicts and mediation is driven in part by other intervening factors. There has been a tremendous increase in the number of independent states in the international system, growing from 66 in 1945 to 155 in 1980 (Correlates of War, 2008). Much of this change is attributable to the process of decolonization, which resulted in virtually all of Africa and parts of Asia being transformed from colonial possessions to multiple, independent states. This affects both the potential for conflict as well as for mediation. An increase in the number of states, *ceteris paribus*, leads to more "opportunities" for war and disputes, even as the likelihood of any one state experiencing such conflict might remain the same.

More states in the international system also means that the pool of potential mediators increases; as states conduct more mediation efforts than either international organizations or regional organizations (see Chapter 3), mediation can increase because there are more actors willing to intervene. Similarly, the growth in international organizations during this period also provides more institutional actors to supply mediation. In 1945, there were only 101 international governmental organizations, whereas by 1980 those numbers swelled to 275 (Pevehouse et al., 2004). Most importantly, the United Nations is now supplemented by other security organizations that can play the role of mediator, including the African Union and the Organization of American States. This effect is felt even more as we move into the end of the Cold and post-Cold War periods. In 2011, for example, representatives of the African Union were deeply involved in efforts to broker an agreement to the political crisis in Ivory Coast. At the same time, the Economic Community of West African States (ECOWAS) threatened to use military force to remove Ivory Coast's incumbent president from power if he did not hand over power to the winner of the country's November 2010 presidential election.

The 1980s saw a decrease in the frequency of both interstate and civil wars, with the number of civil conflicts declining especially sharply, dropping by 58%. At the same time, the number of militarized disputes grew by 48%. The frequency of mediation efforts fell during this decade, but only by 2%. This indicates that mediations are sensitive to "conflict demand," but this demand is not only driven by the highest levels of conflict. Instead, mediation efforts seek to prevent militarized disputes from exploding into full-scale war, and some countervailing influences noted above keep mediations frequent even as the aggregate need declines.

The 1990s represented a sea change in the use of mediation for managing conflicts in the post-World War II world. The number of conflicts increased drastically during the 1990s, rising by 37%, and the largest portion of this increase was driven by a drastic growth in the number of civil wars. Of the sixty-six wars that took place during the 1990s, fifty-nine were internal or intrastate wars (of course many also had an international component as surrounding states intervened, such as in the Second Congo War). During this same period, the number of mediations increased by 469%. In fact, more mediation efforts occurred during the 1990s than during the entire 1945–1989 period!

The sharp increase in the number of mediations was facilitated by several factors. First, the end of the Cold War brought about a period of increased conflict management activity in general. With the UN Security Council no longer tied down by the superpower rivalry and the emergence of an improved working relationship between the United States and Russia, it became easier to muster the international consensus necessary to mediate a wide range of conflicts. The increase in mediation attempts parallels other increases in conflict management techniques. For example, the number of peace operations, many of which were authorized through the United Nations, was dramatically greater in the 1990s as compared to the previous five decades; sixty-one peace operations were initiated by the UN, regional organizations, and multinational groupings during the 1990s as compared to only twenty-nine prior to that period.

Second, the international system saw a significant increase

in the number of democratic states in the so-called "third wave" of democratization. This had twin effects in increasing mediation attempts and indeed all peaceful attempts at conflict management. Strong empirical evidence supports the idea of a democratic peace in which democratic states do not go to war with each other. Accordingly, even when they are engaged in a militarized dispute, they are not likely to escalate their differences to full-scale war. Indeed, evidence suggests that democracies are more likely to employ third-party measures of conflict resolution such as adjudication and, of course, mediation (Dixon, 1993; 1994). Thus, some of the increase in mediation is attributable to states pursuing peaceful resolution of conflicts, avenues that they might not have chosen when they had different regime types. For example, departing from the war-torn history of the former Yugoslavia during the 1990s, Slovenia and Croatia, two new democracies, agreed in 2010 to mediation of their boundary dispute by the European Union.

Democratization in the world also has a significant effect on the conflict behavior of non-democracies. As democratic norms of peaceful conflict resolution spread globally, and this is indicated by the number of democracies in the international system, non-democratic states are also more likely to pursue third-party mediation and related conflict management approaches. Mitchell (2002) found that third-party settlement is sixteen times more likely for two non-democratic states when the proportion of democracies in the system is greater than half as compared to when the proportion is zero. In 2010, both Eritrea and Djibouti, two non-democratic countries, avoided war and accepted mediation of their territorial dispute by Qatar. This joint acceptance of mediation followed a two-year stand-off between the two countries in which Eritrean troops began occupying territory claimed by Djibouti and a brief skirmish between the two sides ensued in 2008.

Thus, the spread of democracy in the world helps account for some of the increase in mediation during this decade.

Changes in Conflict Focus

There has been a notable shift in the frequency of media-tion across conflict types, from a focus on interstate conflict early on to a focus on civil conflict in later decades. From 1945–1979, interstate conflicts experienced decidedly more mediation than civil conflicts, even though civil wars were substantially more frequent than interstate conflicts during each decade. During the 1950s, interstate wars accounted for only 28.6% of all wars during that decade; yet, 81.4% of all mediation efforts during the 1950s were directed toward interstate conflicts. A useful way to compare the differences in the application of mediation is to compare the ratio of the total number of civil conflict mediations during a decade to the total number of civil wars during that decade to a simi-lar ratio for interstate conflicts. During the 1950s, this ratio was more than eleven times larger for interstate conflicts than civil conflicts. Although the disparity between conflict type frequency and mediation rate diminished during the 1960s and 1970s, it still remained substantial; interstate wars repre-sented 21.2% of all wars during the 1960s and 23.1% of them during the 1970s. The mediation–war ratio for interstate wars was about six times larger than that of civil wars during the 1960s and a little less than four times larger during the 1970s. By contrast, 62.9% of mediation efforts during the 1960s and 52.1% of mediations during the 1970s were applied to inter-state conflicts. Consistent with this general tendency, the Yom Kippur War was one of the most frequently mediated conflicts during the 1970s: only the Cyprus Conflict and the Lebanese Civil War attracted more mediation efforts during this period.

Table 2.1 Frequency of Type of Mediation by Decade				
Decade	Civil Conflict Mediation	Civil Conflict Ratio	Interstate Conflict Mediation	Interstate Conflict Ratio
1940s	11 18.97%	1.0	47 81.03%	23.5
1950s	16 18.60%	1.1	70 81.40%	11.7
1960s	76 37.07%	2.9	129 62.93%	18.4
1970s	145 47.85%	3.6	158 52.15%	13.2
1980s	177 59.80%	4.5	119 40.20%	23.8
1990s	1,456 86.46%	24.7	228 13.54%	32.6
Total	1,881 71.47%	9.90	751 28.53%	19.26

Note: Ratio: number of mediation for civil or interstate conflict/number of civil or interstate wars.

This pattern only began to change during the 1980s when, for the first time, the frequency of civil conflict mediation exceeded that of interstate conflict mediation. Even during that time, the mediation rate of civil conflicts was still less than the rate of civil wars themselves. The interstate mediation–war ratio actually spiked upward during the 1980s, rising to more than 5:1. While civil wars constituted 88.6% of all wars during the 1980s, only 59.8% of mediation efforts were directed at civil conflicts.

During the 1980s, the largest number of mediation efforts was devoted to the Lebanese Civil War. Given its long-running history, location in a region of vital strategic interest, and substantial level of involvement in the conflict by other regional powers, the high mediation rate in Lebanon is not surprising.

Interstate conflicts also attracted considerable third-party diplomatic attention. The Iran–Iraq War, no doubt because of its
long duration and deadly character, also attracted a sizeable
share of mediations, particularly from the United Nations.
Other, lower-scale, shorter-lived, interstate conflicts such as
the Falklands War also saw frequent mediation efforts devoted
to them.

During the 1990s, the gap between the percentage of mediations applied to civil conflicts and the percentage of wars that
were intrastate narrowed significantly. During the decade,
89.4% of wars were civil wars and 86.5% of mediations were
focused on civil conflicts. During this decade, the ratio of
mediations to civil wars rose sharply, increasing to over 24:1.
Clearly by the 1990s, the international community had begun
to put more emphasis upon managing civil conflicts.

This shift in conflict management was most readily apparent in the sizeable number of mediation efforts directed at the
civil wars in the former Yugoslavia, Sierra Leone, and Rwanda
during the 1990s. Yet, this shift was not only toward increased
civil war mediation. While there was only one interstate war
during the 1990s, interstate conflicts attracted a total of 228
mediation efforts. As a result, the difference in the ratios of
mediation efforts devoted to interstate and civil conflicts
actually rose from that of the 1980s.

The expansion of civil wars during the 1990s noted above
underscored the need for third-party conflict management
efforts. The civil wars of the 1990s and beyond tended to be
"complex emergencies," which created humanitarian crises
within the states in which they occurred, but also precipitated
negative externalities (e.g. refugees, cross-border fighting) in
neighboring states. These create greater incentives for the
international community to respond proactively to civil conflict, rather than ignoring them because other states pay few
costs associated with their continuance.

In addition, normative changes further help explain why civil wars attracted more international attention in the 1990s and beyond. Historically, state sovereignty was considered a "hard shell" in which governments could do what they wished within their own borders. The development of international human rights law after World War II began to change this conception, but international intervention was still considered a violation of state sovereignty. As we approached the 1990s, the idea that states could launch humanitarian intervention to redress wrongdoing and prevent human rights abuses (Weiss, 2007) gained some traction, if not full legal acceptance. Even more dramatic, the principle of "responsibility to protect" (Bellamy, 2009) extended the idea that the international community had a right to take action to one that made it an obligation. Although these principles relate primarily to military intervention and have not been incorporated fully into international law, they have had a trickle-down effect to the diplomatic realm. States recognize a humanitarian interest in, and moral commitment to, what happens in other countries and believe that it is legitimate to become involved in conflict there; there are no sovereignty barriers to offering mediation assistance, so those barriers do not prevent states, or international organizations of which they are members, from offering their help in resolving conflicts.

Changes in Where Mediators Go

One way to identify the priorities by which mediation efforts are applied is to consider where mediators are sent. Table 2.2 describes the frequency of mediation and conflict by region. Africa and Europe are the two most frequently mediated regions. During the period under study, 36% of all mediations are directed at African conflicts while 23% are directed at European conflicts. Comparing the regional rate of mediation

Table 2.2 Frequency of Mediation, Civil War, and Interstate War by Decade and Region

Decade	Central & South America			Africa			Southwest Asia		
	Mediation	Civil War	Interstate War	Mediation	Civil War	Interstate War	Mediation	Civil War	Interstate War
1940s	8 13.79%	3 27.27%	0 0.00%	0 0.00%	0 0.00%	0 0.00%	8 13.79%	0 0.00%	1 50.00%
1950s	12 13.95%	4 26.67%	0 0.00%	6 6.98%	0 0.00%	1 16.67%	21 24.42%	0 0.00%	0 0.00%
1960s	36 17.56%	2 7.69%	1 14.29%	55 26.83%	11 42.31%	0 0.00%	20 9.76%	0 0.00%	2 28.57%
1970s	11 3.63%	6 15.00%	0 0.00%	113 37.29%	12 30.00%	3 25.00%	0 0.00%	6 15.00%	1 8.33%
1980s	47 15.88%	4 10.26%	1 20.00%	88 29.73%	14 35.90%	1 20.00%	13 4.39%	5 12.82%	0 0.00%
1990s	106 6.29%	3 5.08%	1 14.29%	695 41.27%	29 49.15%	1 14.29%	58 3.44%	4 6.78%	1 14.29%
Total	220 8.36%	22 11.58%	3 7.69%	957 36.36%	66 34.74%	6 15.38%	120 4.56%	15 7.89%	5 12.82%

Table 2.2 (continued)

Decade	East Asia & Pacific			Middle East			Europe		
	Mediation	Civil War	Interstate War	Mediation	Civil War	Interstate War	Mediation	Civil War	Interstate War
1940s	23 39.66%	3 27.27%	0 0.00%	15 25.86%	1 9.09%	1 50.00%	4 6.90%	4 36.36%	0 0.00%
1950s	10 11.63%	8 53.33%	3 50.00%	30 34.88%	2 13.33%	1 16.67%	7 8.14%	1 6.67%	1 16.67%
1960s	40 19.51%	9 34.62%	2 28.57%	54 26.34%	4 15.38%	2 28.57%	0 0.00%	0 0.00%	0 0.00%
1970s	13 4.29%	8 20.00%	5 41.67%	134 44.22%	8 20.00%	2 16.67%	32 10.56%	0 0.00%	1 8.33%
1980s	18 6.08%	8 20.51%	1 20.00%	105 35.47%	7 17.95%	2 40.00%	25 8.45%	1 2.56%	0 0.00%
1990s	97 5.76%	7 11.86%	0 0.00%	180 10.69%	6 10.17%	1 14.29%	548 32.54%	10 16.95%	3 42.86%
Total	201 7.64%	43 22.63%	11 28.21%	518 19.68%	28 14.74%	9 23.08%	616 23.40%	16 8.42%	5 12.82%

against the regional war rate shows clearly that, relative to their conflict propensity, some regions are significantly "over-mediated" while others are "under-mediated." That is, as was demonstrated in the last section, mediation is not wholly driven by conflict opportunity. Other factors are at work, and here we uncover a tendency for mediation provision to vary by region. For example, Europe's share of mediation efforts is more than three times its share of all global conflict.

Other regions receive substantially less attention from mediators relative to their proportion of conflicts. The East Asia/Pacific region is especially under-mediated. Its share of mediation is less than a third of its share of world conflict. This might not be surprising given the limited organizational capacity for conflict management in that geographic area. The East Asia/Pacific region has only the Asia–Pacific Economic Cooperation (APEC) as an organization that ties together all the states in the region. Yet that organization is still loosely constructed and has concentrated on economic matters (and not security concerns). Subregionally, North Asia lacks any kind of regional international organization that could facilitate mediation or other conflict management approaches; as such, controlling conflict in that region has more often relied on traditional deterrence strategies involving alliances (Cha, 2003). The South Asian Association for Regional Cooperation (SAARC) has an explicit provision in its charter prohibiting its involvement in bilateral and "contentious" issues (Bajpai, 2003). The Association of Southeast Asian States (ASEAN) has been less formally constrained, but still reluctant to involve itself in security matters among members, such as competing claims and confrontations over the Spratly Islands.

The Central/South American region also draws less mediation than one would expect, given its conflict frequency. Although the Central/South America region accounts for 10.9% of all global conflicts, it only receives 8.4% of all mediation efforts during this time. Direct diplomatic efforts (Shaw, 2003) have often been successful, fostered by a regional norm of peaceful resolution. Accordingly, fewer mediation attempts in that region might be more indicative of conflict management, and the lesser need for third-party intervention.

Mapping the frequency of mediation by region against the frequency of conflict over time also points to some clear patterns in the application of mediation. Looking decade by decade, both Europe and the Middle East are the two most consistently over-mediated regions, relative to their total share of system conflict. Although Europe's share of mediation from 1945–1949 is significantly less than its share of total conflict, this pattern begins to shift in the following decades. During the 1950s and 1960s, Europe's share of mediation is roughly commensurate with its share of total conflict. During the 1970s, Europe experiences more than five times more mediation than its share of global conflict would predict. A similar gap between conflict and mediation shares holds for Europe during the 1980s. Only during the 1990s does this disparity begin to wane. This decrease, however, is a result of a substantial increase in the amount of conflict experienced by Europe, not a decrease in the amount of mediation devoted to Europe. In fact, during the 1990s, 32.5% of all mediation efforts are directed at the region. During the Cold War period, much of the focus on the continent could be attributed to the desire to avoid severe conflict or escalation that might prompt a direct superpower confrontation and activate the NATO and Warsaw Pact alliances. Later, the close economic ties between European states and the network of international organizations in the region, with the European Union at the center, provided the incentives and the mechanisms for enhanced conflict management (Duffield, 2003).

The Middle East also shows a similar tendency toward over-mediation. Although the gap between its portion of global mediation and conflict is less than that of Europe, the Middle East's share of mediation is at least 44% higher than its proportion of conflict during every decade from 1945 to 1989, peaking during the 1970s when the region draws 44.2% of all mediation while only experiencing 19.2% of all conflicts. Only during the 1990s does this pattern change, at which time the Middle East actually attracts mediator attention equal to its frequency of conflict. In contrast to Europe, this concentration is not a function of numerous and effective security organizations in the region; in fact, various groupings such as the League of Arab States and the Gulf Cooperation Council have been notably ineffective in regional conflicts, and especially irrelevant in the central conflict in the area – the Arab–Israeli conflict and all its permutations. Instead, this region has primarily attracted external mediation attempts, from states such as Romania, Norway, and most obviously the United States. Yet similar to Europe, the risk of escalation and the threat of superpower involvement have put a premium on conflict management there. The Middle East has long been a "shatter-belt" in which major power competition has played out. Close ties between the USA and Israel on one hand and the Soviet Union and Egypt (as well as Syria) on the other meant that any major dispute or war ran the risk of a broader conflict, much as any European conflict had the strong likelihood of superpower intervention. Thus, mediation efforts here and in Europe were motivated not only by the *frequency* of conflict but also by the *potential for escalation*.

Similarly, the divergence between conflict share and mediator attention highlights the role which third-party interests play in shaping where mediation is used. The occurrence of mediation is significantly influenced by the characteristics of the conflict with third parties becoming more likely to offer mediation when conflict becomes intense, conditions on the battlefield deteriorate, or political shifts occur among the parties that create an opening for diplomacy (Regan and Stam, 2000; Greig, 2005). At the same time, third parties are strategic not only in terms of when they offer mediation, but also where they offer it. In this respect, that the Middle East and Europe, two of the most strategically important regions of the world, receive more mediation than their level of conflict would predict is consistent with the idea that third parties tend to direct mediation toward those conflicts about which they care most.

Repeated Mediations

The priorities that third parties set in their usage of mediation are evident by looking at where they devote their greatest energies. To a significant extent, we have identified these by reference to the kinds of conflict and geographic patterns in mediation over time. Yet another way that priorities are evident is by reference to repeated mediations, that is, conflicts in which there is more than one mediation attempt, often by the same actor(s). A conflict in which a third party provides repeated mediation efforts signals a clear interest by the mediator in the conflict, the parties involved in it, and its management.

Table 2.3 lists the conflicts that have experienced the most mediation attempts. These are predominantly internationalized civil wars with significant casualties. It is perhaps not surprising that conflicts with the greatest severity and those that are protracted are those that attract the most international attention. Yet these cases also reveal a pattern of international intervention from neighboring states with a potential for further conflict expansion and escalation. For example, civil war in the former Yugoslavia not only brought in Serb and Croat forces from outside but ran the risk of engulfing other former Yugoslav republics and NATO forces, beyond the latter's

Rank	Conflict	Mediation Frequency
Table 2.3 Most Frequently Mediated Conflicts		
1	Yugoslavian Civil War: The Balkans War	274
2	Angola–South Africa: Intervention and Civil War	99
3	Azerbaijan–Armenia: Nagorno-Karabakh Conflict	95
4	The Second Lebanese Civil War	80
5	The USSR–Afghanistan: Intervention and Civil War	79
6	Liberia–Sierra Leone: Intervention and the Sierra Leone Civil War	73
7	Kosovo War	72
10	Georgia–South Ossetia: Abkhazia Secession War	66
10	Rwandan Invasion	66
10	The Cyprus Conflict: Invasion and Partition	66

limited role. Mediation tends to be attracted to the most serious conflicts, and these are not easily resolved. Accordingly, and perhaps desirably, the international community makes repeated efforts in these instances.

Table 2.4 describes the frequency of mediation efforts by the same mediator in a conflict. A significant number (64.7%) of mediation efforts are only carried out by a particular mediator once. Some of these efforts occur only once because the third party is able to manage or resolve the conflict. The Organization of American States led a successful one-time mediation effort in 1992 to resolve the guerilla insurgency in Suriname. Other one-time mediation efforts are less successful, with the occurrence of follow-on mediation limited by either an unwillingness of the parties to talk again or a lack of interest by the third party. Neither the mediation by President Soglo of Benin in the 1994 Ghana–Togo border dispute nor the effort by Syrian Foreign Minister Qaddor in the 1992

Table 2.4 Number of Repeat Mediation Efforts by Same Mediator by Type of Conflict

	0	1	2	3	4	5	6+
Civil conflict	1,200 63.80%	288 15.31%	125 6.65%	70 3.72%	45 2.39%	33 1.75%	120 6.38%
Interstate conflict	502 66.84%	116 15.45%	56 7.46%	26 3.46%	16 2.13%	9 1.20%	26 3.46%
Total	1,702 64.67%	404 15.35%	181 6.88%	96 3.65%	61 2.32%	42 1.60%	146 5.55%

border dispute over the Hala'ib Triangle between Egypt and Sudan was successful. Yet, these mediation efforts were not followed by further third-party diplomacy by either that third party or a different one.

In this respect, both wholly negative and positive mediation outcomes push against repeated mediation efforts by the same party in an individual conflict. If a mediation effort fails and the third party sees few fruits from its labors, it will be unlikely to offer future mediation. At the same time, if a third party is successful in producing a mediated settlement to a conflict, there is less need for future mediation by the third party, as long as the conflict remains settled. Instead, it is those mediation efforts that fall in the middle ground between these two extremes that tend to prompt repeated mediations. When progress in diplomacy is being made but important issues remain unsettled, a mediator will often take up the task again hoping to build on the progress already made. The disputants are often receptive to such renewals, given not only the progress, but also that trust and the diplomatic processes have already been established with the extant mediator rather than having to start over with a new third party. It might also be the case that a third party has a sufficient stake in the outcome of a conflict to stick with mediation in spite of previous failures.

There are important differences in the issues and barriers to settlement faced by civil and interstate conflicts. For example, many of the most intense interstate conflicts occur over territorial disputes. Ethnic conflicts often comprise the most violent form of civil conflicts. Territorial conflicts, because disputed territory can be divided between the sides, can often be more amenable to diplomatic settlement than ethnic conflicts. Ethnic conflicts, such as those fought over religious beliefs, are significantly less divisible and more problematic for settlement because of their immutability (Svensson, 2007c) and the intangibility of the stakes.

The challenges inherent to mediating civil wars are not confined only to ethnic conflicts. Unlike most interstate conflicts, the competing sides challenge the legitimacy of one another in civil conflicts. As a result, governments often refuse dialogue with rebel groups in order to avoid appearing to grant legitimacy to the rebels. This creates an additional difficult challenge for a third party seeking to bring a government and a rebel group to the bargaining table to negotiate a settlement to the conflict. If one side refuses to talk to another, a diplomatic settlement to a conflict becomes demonstrably harder.

Given these differences in the issues and barriers to settlement faced by civil wars, it would be reasonable to expect that civil and interstate conflicts will show different tendencies toward repeated mediation, and indeed this is the case. Civil conflicts show a greater propensity for repeated mediation. In fact, among the conflicts receiving the largest number of mediation efforts by the same mediator, most were civil conflicts. For example, beginning in 1995, Burundi saw the most frequent sustained diplomatic intervention by a third party of any conflict in our data, attracting twenty-six mediation efforts by former Tanzanian President Nyerere. Following Nyerere's death in 1999, his conflict management efforts were continued by South African President Mandela. This process ultimately produced an agreement between the two sides in 2000. Yet, we see little evidence that repeated mediation is carried out by the same mediator. Both civil and interstate conflicts have similar tendencies against repeated mediation by the same mediator. The majority of mediation efforts in civil and interstate conflicts, 63.8% and 66.8% respectively, are conducted by a first-time mediator to the conflict. The similarity in rates holds across all but the highest levels of previous mediation activity. Nearly 6.4% of civil conflicts are mediated six or more times by the same mediator. By contrast, only about 3.5% of interstate conflicts attract this same level of repeated mediator activity.

Examining the distribution of repeated mediator behavior by region in Table 2.5 shows some clear distinctions in the focus of mediators upon particular regions. Across all regions, the majority of mediations are conducted by a third party mediating the conflict for the first time. The prevalence of one-shot mediation is less pronounced in Europe and Central/South America, with only slightly more than 50% of regional mediations being conducted by a third party intervening for the first time. If we look at the occurrence of high-density interventions by the same mediator in conflicts in Europe and Central/South America, their regional distinctiveness becomes even more pronounced.

Among European conflicts, the conflicts in Cyprus and the former Yugoslavia stand out as those showing repeated mediation by the same third party. In Cyprus, UN Secretary General Perez de Cueller alone accounted for twenty-eight separate mediation efforts. British diplomat Lord Owen was involved in over thirty mediation attempts during the civil war in the former Yugoslavia. In Central America, UN diplomat Jean Arnault led fourteen mediation efforts between rebels and the Guatemalan government during the 1990s. These sustained mediation efforts are important because they allow

Table 2.5 Number of Repeat Mediation Efforts by Same Mediator by Region							
	0	1	2	3	4	5	6+
Central & South America	115 52.27%	37 16.82%	19 8.64%	13 5.91%	10 4.55%	6 2.73%	20 9.09%
Africa	672 70.22%	142 14.84%	55 5.75%	27 2.82%	13 1.36%	10 1.04%	38 3.97%
Southwest Asia	78 65.00%	19 15.83%	9 7.50%	5 4.17%	3 2.50%	2 1.67%	4 3.33%
East Asia & Pacific	152 75.62%	28 13.93%	11 5.47%	5 2.49%	4 1.99%	1 0.50%	0 0.00%
Middle East	347 66.99%	84 16.22%	41 7.92%	14 2.70%	8 1.54%	5 0.97%	19 3.67%
Europe	338 54.87%	94 15.26%	46 7.47%	32 5.19%	23 3.73%	18 2.92%	65 10.55%
Total	1,702 64.67%	404 15.35%	181 6.88%	96 3.65%	61 2.32%	42 1.60%	146 5.55%

a third party to develop relationships with the conflicting sides and build trust with them. In turn, this tends to make third parties more effective mediators, increasing the prospects for a mediated settlement over time.

The rate of recurring mediation is quite low in Africa, Southwest Asia, East Asia/Pacific, and the Middle East. On average, only 5.6% of all mediations in these regions are conducted by a mediator who has previously mediated a specific conflict at least four times. Within Central/South America, however, 16.4% of all mediations are conducted by a mediator intervening in a conflict four or more times. Similarly, 17.2% of all mediations in European conflicts are conducted by a mediator that has previously mediated the conflict at least four times. This pattern suggests two insights. First, as was the case in the application of mediation in general, Europe is the focus of considerable mediation activity; it receives more than its share of mediation and it is more likely to attract repeated efforts by the same third party. Second, although Central/South America draws less than its expected share of mediation as a function of its proportion of world conflict, when its conflicts are mediated, they are more likely to draw sustained mediation efforts by the third party. Many of these repeated mediation efforts in Central/South America are conducted by the Organization of American States, suggesting that the presence of a regional organization supported by a major power that is deeply involved in managing local conflicts encourages high-density mediation of conflicts.

Although repeated mediation efforts by the same third party can signal the commitment a particular actor has toward managing a conflict, the presence of repeated mediation in the same conflict by different parties can also underscore both the strategic importance of the conflict and the difficulties that third parties face in managing it. In general, those conflicts that draw the attention of multiple third parties, each taking their own initiative to manage the conflict, are those that are likely to be the most significant security threats to the international community, the gravest threats to civilians, or a combination of the two. The history of mediation during the conflict in the former Yugoslavia is consistent with this pattern. This conflict drew frequent and repeated mediation efforts from several third parties, including representatives of the European Community, the United States, and the United Nations. Combined, these mediation efforts made the conflicts in the former Yugoslavia the most heavily mediated conflicts in the post-World War II era, attracting nearly three times as many mediation attempts as the second most mediated conflict during this period. In this respect, multiple parties are willing to provide mediation to these conflicts because they are seen as the cases where conflict management is most urgent. At the same time, these conflicts are also typically the most difficult to settle. As a result, they face a cycle of different mediators, each attempting to successfully manage the conflict where others have failed.

The Sierra Leone Civil War is a good example of the revolving door character of mediator involvement in some conflicts. During the course of the war, fifty-five different mediators and mediation teams intervened diplomatically. These mediators ran the gamut of third parties, ranging from US Secretary of State Madeleine Albright to Libyan leader Muammar Gaddafi. Several regional organizations were also involved in mediating the conflict, including the Arab League, ECOWAS, and the Intergovernmental Authority on Development (IGAD). All total, the conflict in Sierra Leone experienced seventy-three mediations from 1991 to 1999. Several factors were key influences on the high frequency of mediation of the Sierra Leone conflict. Not only was the conflict long-running and bloody, but it was linked to the conflict in neighboring Liberia and produced hundreds of thousands of refugees that spilled across the country's borders. These characteristics showed the need for conflict management and provided the interest necessary for third parties to intervene diplomatically. At the same time, the need for the intervention of so many mediators in the conflict also underscores the intractability of the Sierra Leone Conflict.

Table 2.6 describes the distribution of mediation efforts in conflicts by different third parties. Here we see the impact of both strategic interests and conflict management difficulty on the number of different mediators that intervene in conflicts. On average, a civil conflict attracts mediation from more than three times as many different third parties as an interstate conflict. This is consistent with the challenge that civil conflicts present for conflict management. Although both civil and interstate conflicts are important threats to international security, settlements tend to be more difficult to achieve

Table 2.6 Number of Different Mediators per Conflict					
	Mean	Median	Minimum	Maximum	Standard Deviation
Type of Conflict					
Civil conflict	17.77	11	1	135	22.88
Interstate conflict	5.04	3	1	66	7.74
Location of Conflict					
Central & South America	4.29	1.5	1	28	5.56
Africa	13.53	5	1	100	18.87
Southwest Asia	8.23	3	1	24	8.82
East Asia & Pacific	8.14	3	1	36	9.58
Middle East	7.49	3	1	57	11.12
Europe	24.21	5	1	135	37.65
Total	10.15	3	1	135	16.83

and less durable in civil wars (Walter, 2002; Downes, 2004; Toft, 2010), making mediation less likely to be successful and opening up the possibility for new third parties to intervene diplomatically.

Examining the average number of unique mediators applied per conflict by region again exemplifies some significant disparities from region to region. On average, a conflict in Central/South America only receives the assistance of 4.3 mediators, the lowest of any region. Although they had a low rate of repeated mediation by the same mediator, African conflicts have a much higher frequency of different mediators; they are each mediated by an average of 13.5 mediators, the second highest of any region. Comparing these findings with those of Table 2.5 suggests that African conflicts, rather than drawing the sustained focus of a single mediator that is likely to build a relationship with the parties over time and increase their prospects of achieving a settlement, instead face a revolving door of different mediators. The reasons why particular mediators might volunteer (or not) for particular conflicts are addressed in detail in Chapter 3.

Here again, Europe is the stand-out region in terms of mediator attention. European conflicts not only draw the sustained efforts of individual mediators, making them more likely to be mediated by the same third party several times, but they also attract a larger number of unique mediators than any other region. On average, European conflicts are mediated by an average of 24.2 different mediators. This is nearly double the average of African conflicts and more than triple that of the other four regions. This distribution of mediator attention seems likely to benefit European conflicts by providing a diversity of mediators that may each bring different resources, skills, and capabilities to the diplomatic process without detracting from the effect that the development of a relationship with an individual mediator over a sustained period of diplomacy has upon the prospects for settlement.

Barriers to Entry: Why Some Conflicts Resist Mediation

Mediation is an extensively used diplomatic tool for dealing with conflicts in the international system. Indeed, most conflicts, both civil and international, attract at least one mediation effort at some point during the conflict. All total, about 72% of all conflicts experience mediation during their lifespan. Despite this high rate of activity, there are a number of important barriers to entry that at least some conflicts face that limit the occurrence of mediation. Some such barriers are tied to the characteristics of the belligerents involved in the conflict and the features of the conflict itself. Others are linked to the level of interest in a conflict held by third parties considering intervention in the conflict. Put together, these barriers to entry play a key role in the 28% of all conflicts that experience no mediation at all.

Because mediation is consensual, the parties in a conflict are only likely to accept mediation when they expect to benefit from participation in the diplomatic effort. For some parties, there may be few benefits to accepting mediation. Major powers, for example, often see little benefit from accepting mediation, making them less likely to accept third-party offers of diplomacy (Princen, 1992; Greig, 2005). Although third parties can assist actors in producing an agreement by offering incentives to sweeten potential deals or by offering to guarantee and monitor the implementation of an agreement, few third parties are likely to have the resources necessary to do so in conflicts involving a major power. Instead, major powers are more likely to see the addition of an outside mediator as interfering with or limiting their options for settling the conflict on their own terms.

Comparing the mediation rate of major power conflicts to minor power conflicts illustrates this logic. Among minor power conflicts, nearly 80% experience mediation. This figure drops significantly among major powers, with fewer than half of all major power conflicts drawing mediation. Consistent with this tendency among major powers, both China and the United States have tended to avoid mediation of their conflicts. None of China's conflicts over the Spratly Islands, its dispute with the Philippines in 1995, or its clash with Vietnam in 1988, were mediated. Similarly, no mediation occurred in the period prior to the US invasion of Panama to remove Manuel Noriega from power in 1989. In each case, there was little that a third party could offer to entice the major power toward mediation.

This is not to say that major powers can never see the benefits of mediation in their conflict. Algeria, for example, played a critical role mediating between the United States and Iran during the Iranian Hostage Crisis. Algeria served as a go-between to a superpower and regional power, both of whom were considerably more powerful than she was. Because the United States and Iran had broken diplomatic relations with one another and had few communication links, Algeria, as a state trusted by both sides, played a vital role communicating between the two sides. The Algerian diplomacy ultimately yielded the 1981 Algiers Accords that released the American hostages. In this case, Algerian diplomatic assistance was seen as beneficial by both the USA and Iran because Algeria could provide a unique service to the two sides: a trustworthy means of communications.

Beyond the characteristics of the conflicting parties, the development of their conflict also has consequences for the likelihood of mediation. The severity of a conflict, for example, can be a double-edged sword for the willingness of the parties in conflict to join a mediation effort. On the one hand, as the severity of a conflict increases, the level of hostility between the two sides grows, making them less willing to compromise and closing off communication links. As a result, as conflict severity increases, parties in conflict become less likely to accept mediation (Bercovitch et al., 1991). On the other hand, while conflict severity heightens animosity, it also imposes costs on the two sides. As these costs grow, the willingness of the disputants to continue to pay these costs and suffer the pain produced by a conflict diminishes, increasing their willingness to turn toward to diplomatic solutions such as mediation (Regan and Stam, 2000; Zartman, 2000; Greig, 2001). In this respect, a key point in a conflict is the transition point at which conflict costs begin to exert a stronger push toward compromise than the pull toward continued violence caused by the hostility that intense conflict produces. Of course, for mediation to happen, not only must the disputants be willing to participate, but a third party must be willing to play the role of mediator. Who mediates and what motivations drive mediators is the subject of analysis in the next chapter.

The Chittagong Hill Tracts Conflict in Bangladesh is a good example of the type of conflict that tends to go unmediated. Although this civil conflict between the government of Bangladesh and the indigenous people of the Chittagong Hill Tracts produced a relatively small number of casualties, it lasted for twenty years and produced human rights abuses by both sides. Yet, with few direct interests at stake for other states, there was little incentive for outside powers to seek to broker a settlement to the conflict. As a result, the war continued without attracting any mediation efforts until the two sides eventually reached an agreement themselves.

Conclusions

In this chapter we have traced the ways in which mediation is applied to conflicts in the international system. Over time, the use of mediation to deal with conflicts across the globe has exploded. Whereas mediation tended to be sparsely used during the 1940s and 1950s, its use has increased over time, dramatically so with the close of the twentieth century, mediation from 1990 to 1999 alone being more frequent than for all prior decades combined. This growth of mediation during the 1990s is good news as the global community increasingly confronts more deadly and intractable conflicts that cause significant levels of civilian suffering and a heightened risk of spilling across borders.

Although the use of mediation has expanded, we have seen that mediation is applied neither randomly nor uniformly. Instead, conflicts in some regions such as Europe and the

Middle East are more likely to attract mediation than conflicts in East Asia. Mediation efforts are also not uniformly distributed between civil and interstate conflicts. During the early portion of the post-World War II era, the lion's share of mediation efforts was focused on interstate conflicts. The application of mediation has shifted over time, with civil conflicts increasingly seeing more attention from mediators. This is a welcome development, as the threat of civil conflicts has grown over the last few decades while the frequency of interstate conflicts has receded. Nevertheless, civil conflicts continue to attract a smaller share of mediation efforts than their prevalence would suggest. The strength of the sovereignty norm and the principle of non-interference in the internal affairs of other states explain some of the under-mediation of civil conflicts. The strong barriers to negotiated settlement that are common to civil wars also explain some of the reduced share of civil conflict mediation. Combined, these forces tend to postpone serious mediation of many civil conflicts until deep into their lifespan, perhaps when mediation is likely to be significantly more difficult and less effective.

In the next chapter, we will look at who provides mediation to conflicts in the international system. We will explore what interests tend to drive their willingness to intervene diplomatically in conflicts, distinguishing between the effects of more altruistic intentions such as humanitarian concerns and the strategic interests of third parties.

CHAPTER THREE

The Providers of Mediation

In the previous chapter, we identified wide divergence in the application of mediation to conflicts in the international system as well as the ways in which the use of mediation has changed over time. Some regions with fewer conflicts attract substantially more third-party conflict management efforts than regions with more violence. Interstate conflicts continue to attract substantially more mediator attention than civil conflicts, although this gap has narrowed over time. In order to understand the ways in which mediation is employed in the international system, it is essential to recognize a fundamental difference between mediation and other conflict management tools. Unlike bilateral negotiations, mediation requires the availability of a willing outside party to assist the belligerents in managing their conflict. Although this third party might be neutral in the dispute, it must have sufficient interest in the conflict, the parties, or the effects of the conflict to be willing to offer its help to the two sides. Unlike military intervention aimed at undermining the capacity of one or more sides to continue fighting, mediation also requires the consent of the contending sides. Not only is participation in a mediation process voluntary for the parties in conflict, the two sides also retain the power to reject any proposed settlement that is developed during the talks. In this respect, the occurrence of mediation requires the combination of both a third party sufficiently motivated to offer mediation and belligerents willing to accept an offer of mediation by a specific third party.

61

In this chapter, we examine who provides mediation to conflicts in the international system and the forces that motivate them to do so. Understanding these motivating forces will allow us to understand why some conflicts tend to draw frequent and sustained attention from mediators, sometimes from more than one, and why others go without mediation entirely. Although mediators are often stereotypically seen as neutral and disinterested parties, we argue that this is rarely the case in international mediation. Third parties often have important interests at stake in the conflicts in which they provide mediation. Without these interests, they would be unlikely to offer mediation in the first place. As part of this discussion, we look at which actors tend to be the leading providers of mediation, the ways in which multiple third parties can work together to mediate a conflict, and how third parties find a balance between providing mediation to those conflicts that need mediation the most, such as those marked by genocide and refugee flows, and those in which the third party has the greatest stakes.

Providers of Mediation on the International Stage

A diverse group of third parties provide mediation to both civil and interstate conflicts. The pool of mediators includes individuals, states, non-governmental organizations (NGOs), and regional and global organizations. Table 3.1 provides a summary overview of mediation participation by actor, broken down further by decade.

As we noted in Chapter 2, there is a dramatic increase in mediation attempts in the 1990s, but the patterns in actor participation are relatively consistent over the six decades. International organizations (IOs) and states lead the way overall and within each time period. On a relative basis, Figure 3.1

Table 3.1 Total Mediation Efforts by Third Party and Decade							
Identity	1940s	1950s	1960s	1970s	1980s	1990s	Total
Individuals	2	1	6	4	12	61	86
IGOs	37	50	123	130	128	636	1,104
NGOs	0	0	8	13	18	69	108
States	17	33	63	141	124	633	1,011
Mixed	2	2	5	15	14	281	319
Unspecified	0	0	0	0	0	4	4
Total	58	86	205	303	296	1,684	2,632

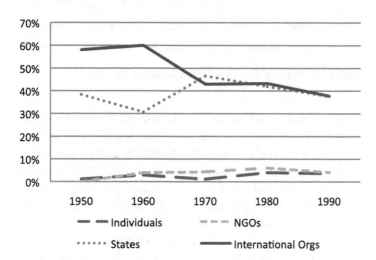

Figure 3.1 Share of Mediation Efforts over Time by Provider

shows the share of total mediation activity during the period of study by type of third party. States, as the dominant actor in the international system, have been the most frequent provider of conflict mediation, accounting for more than 38% of all mediation efforts. Among states, the five major powers (United States, United Kingdom, France, Russia/

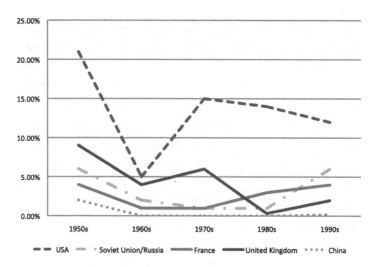

Figure 3.2 Share of Total Mediation by Major Powers

Soviet Union, and China) have accounted for about 50% of all state-conducted mediation efforts during this period. Over time, we see a slight shift in the providers of state-conducted mediation away from major powers as mediation becomes more frequent. During the 1950s, major powers conducted 61% of all state-conducted mediation efforts. By the 1990s, this share had been diminished slightly, with major power mediations comprising 55% of total state mediation.

State mediation by the major powers reflects the influence of both their shared and individual interests on their diplomatic activity. Figure 3.2 tracks the share of mediation by major powers throughout the post-World War II era. Apart from China, the other major powers participated in multiple mediation efforts during the civil war in the former Yugoslavia and in the conflict in Kosovo during the 1990s. Given the threat that both of those conflicts posed for spreading and drawing in other participants, both wars presented compelling cases for mediation by the major powers. Outside of these conflicts, each major power also directed significant portions of its mediation activity to conflicts in which it had more specific interests. For the United States, this has meant focusing considerable mediation attention on conflicts in the Middle East, particularly the enduring rivalry between Israel and Egypt and the conflict between Israel and Lebanon during the 1980s. The United States also provided frequent mediation efforts between Angola and South Africa during the South African intervention in the Angolan Civil War.

Among states, the United States has been the most active provider of state mediation since 1945. All total, the United States has been involved in slightly more than 12% of all mediation efforts and nearly 32% of all state mediations since World War II. The high watermark for American mediation efforts occurred during the 1950s, arguably at the apex of the American global power position, when the United States participated in 21% of all mediation efforts. American mediation dropped off sharply during the 1960s before rebounding to a relatively stable mediation participation rate around 13% during 1970–1999. This figure, because it only reflects state mediation, underestimates the overall level of American involvement as a provider of conflict management because it excludes mediation efforts conducted by organizations such as the UN and the OAS that are encouraged and supported by the United States. This high level of American mediation activity reflects the broad array of interests it holds throughout the world and its capacity to bring resources to bear to the conflicts in which it serves as a mediator.

Russian/Soviet mediation activity has historically been less frequent, about one third of that of the USA, accounting for about 4% of all global mediation activity. During the Soviet era, mediation by the Soviet Union peaked during the 1950s at about 6% of all mediation activity as the superpowers

competed for influence across the globe, but dropped off
sharply through the 1980s. After the fall of the Soviet Union,
the frequency and share of mediation conducted by Russia
increased during the 1990s, rising to represent 6% of all
global mediation. Of the 114 Russian/Soviet mediation efforts,
101 took place during the 1990s. This increase in Russian
mediation reflected the emergence of nearby destabilizing
threats to Russian security in both the former Yugoslavia and
in some of the former Soviet republics.

During the 1970s and 1980s, the Soviet Union focused its
small number of mediation efforts on global hotspots such
as the Arab–Israeli conflicts, the civil war in Cambodia, and
the conflict in Cyprus. During the 1990s, Russian mediation
efforts were largely redirected to conflicts in its "near abroad"
and nearby. As a result, Russia engaged in numerous mediation efforts over the breakaway regions of South Ossetia and
Abkhazia in Georgia as well as during the Nagorno-Karabakh
conflict between Armenia and Azerbaijan. Indeed, Russian
mediation in these two conflicts alone during the 1990s
accounted for one third of all Russian/Soviet mediation
during the entire post-World War II period. The proximity
of each of these conflicts to Russia, their shared history with
Russia during the Soviet era, and, in the case of Georgia,
the presence of a significant number of ethnic Russians in
the conflict zones each provided a significant incentive for
Russian diplomatic involvement in the conflicts.

Similar to the Russians, historical linkages also influenced
where Britain and France devoted significant portions of
their diplomatic interventions. For France, this has meant
considerable mediation activity in the civil wars involving its
former colonial holdings in Cambodia, Niger, and Lebanon,
to name a few. British mediation activity has been somewhat
more broadly applied, although Britain has still devoted considerable diplomatic energy to conflicts involving its former

colonies. In particular, Britain has directed frequent mediation efforts at its former colonial territories in Zimbabwe and
Cyprus.

Among the major powers, China is the outlier in terms of
mediation activity. In the last five decades of the twentieth century, China only engaged in five mediation efforts. Four (two
of which occurred during the 1950s) were conflicts involving
China's regional neighbors. These diplomatic interventions
dealt with the independence movement in French Indochina
during the 1950s as well as the Cambodian Civil War and the
conflict between India and Pakistan over Kashmir during the
1990s. China's limited activity as a mediator is a function of
its lack of former colonies, its recent rise as a major power,
and its professed doctrine of non-interference, each of which
undermines its opportunities for diplomatic intervention. As
Chinese power grows over time and takes a more prominent
role on the global stage, it makes sense to expect to see an
increase in Chinese mediation activity, including in conflicts
outside its region. In fact, China's effort in 1999 to mediate the civil war in Djibouti may reflect an initial step in this
direction.

Although mediation conducted by states has played an
important role in managing both civil and interstate conflicts,
international organizations (IOs) have also played an important role as a provider of third-party diplomacy. International
organizations such as the United Nations, African Union,
Organization of American States, and Arab League have
accounted for a sizeable share of global mediation activity. Mediation activity by international organizations peaked
immediately after World War II during the 1940s and 1950s
when it accounted for 60% of all mediation efforts in the
international system. IO mediation, however, has declined
fairly steady over the last three decades of the twentieth century, dropping to only 38% of all mediations during the 1990s.

Mediation by the United Nations, in particular, has followed the same declining trend. During the 1940s and 1950s, the UN was involved in 49% of all mediation attempts in the international system. By the 1990s, the UN share of mediation had dropped to about 34%. Still, the United Nations has played an active role in mediating some of the world's most dangerous trouble spots, including high-profile flashpoints between Israel and Lebanon, and India and Pakistan. The United Nations, however, has devoted its greatest attention to civil conflicts, directing more than one third of its 888 post-World War II mediation efforts to just four conflicts: the civil war in the former Yugoslavia, the conflict in Cyprus, Angola's civil war, and the Western Sahara conflict respectively. Although the share of UN mediation has diminished across time, its total mediation activity has risen dramatically over the last few decades. During the 1950s, the United Nations participated in only thirty-nine mediation efforts. During the 1990s, the level of UN mediation activity increased more than fourteen-fold, with the UN engaging in 569 mediations during the ten-year period. In this respect, the decline in the relative share of total global mediation activity conducted by the UN is a function of the dramatic rise in the overall application of mediation, rather than a diminution of the provision of mediation by the UN.

Although UN mediation accounts for 64% of all mediation activity by international organizations, several other international organizations have been leading providers of conflict mediation in the international system. IO activity has increased over time as the capacity of regional organizations for diplomacy and other forms of conflict management has also increased. The Organization for African Unity (OAU, the forerunner of today's African Union) was among the most active international organizations in providing mediation, intervening in some of its region's most deadly and intractable conflicts. The OAU devoted its largest share of mediation attention to Burundi's civil war, but also provided frequent mediation efforts to civil wars in the Comoros, Liberia, and Rwanda as well. The Organization for Security and Cooperation in Europe (OSCE) was also an active mediator during the 1990s, devoting the largest fraction of its mediation efforts to the conflict between Azerbaijan and Armenia over Nagorno-Karabakh. Large regional organizations, such as the OSCE and OAU, benefit from the combination of their broad-based membership; they can increase leverage during mediation if a consensus for diplomatic intervention exists among members, and they also have first-hand familiarity with the regions in which they operate.

Mediation of conflicts in the international system is not solely the responsibility of states and the international organizations that they create. Both non-governmental organizations and private individuals have played a small role as mediation providers, each accounting for 4% and 3%, respectively, of all mediation activity. The Catholic Church has been an especially active provider of mediation. Its mediation activity between Chile and Argentina during the Beagle Channel Crisis was decisive in bringing the two sides back from the brink of war and establishing a framework for the eventual settlement of the conflict and establishment of a long-term peace. The International Red Cross has also mediated civil conflicts in Somalia, the Dominican Republic, and Sierra Leone. Smaller religious groups such as the Quakers have likewise played a role in mediating civil conflicts ranging from Sri Lanka to Nigeria. For the Quakers, their provision of mediation is driven by their philosophy, which sees war as inherently wrong and encourages concrete action in the name of peace. These religious beliefs, in turn, often serve to encourage trust of Quaker mediators by warring parties who see Quaker motivation for providing mediation as rooted in their pacifist and spiritual beliefs (Bercovitch and Kadayifci-Orellana, 2009).

Private individuals have also played a role in mediating conflicts in the international system. The pool of private mediators is often drawn from individuals with significant experience in government service, leadership in religious organizations, or key positions within prominent international organizations. Former US President Jimmy Carter, former South African President Nelson Mandela, former UN Secretary-General Kofi Annan, and Anglican Archbishop Desmond Tutu have all served as mediators to conflicts throughout the world. Private mediation efforts have been significantly less frequent than mediation by states and international organizations, accounting for slightly more than 3% of all mediation activity during the post-World War II period. This share of mediation activity by private individuals has been largely unchanged over time. Private individuals rely extensively on their personal prestige and diplomatic skills given that they lack the resources and elements of material power that would allow them to offer carrots and sticks to the disputants, or to provide any guarantee to the parties for any settlement that might be reached.

The two most active private mediators during the post-World War II period have been former Tanzanian President Julius Nyerere and former US President Jimmy Carter. Nyerere's mediation activity was directed at the civil war in his native country's neighbor, Burundi. Throughout the Burundi conflict, Nyerere was involved in at least seventeen separate mediation efforts to manage the conflict. Jimmy Carter's mediation activity has been more broad-based. He has been involved in mediating the war between Ethiopia and Eritrea, the 1994 crisis in Haiti, and, working alongside Archbishop Tutu and former President Nyerere, the Burundi Civil War. Carter also brokered the 1995 Guinea Worm Ceasefire during the Sudan Civil War, allowing relief workers access to portions of Sudan hard-hit by Guinea worm and other diseases during the conflict.

Multiparty Mediation

Mediation efforts are often conducted by a single mediator that focuses its energies on managing the conflict. This can be beneficial because the more the belligerents build a rapport and develop trust with a third party, the more effective that third party can be in mediating the conflict. This is why conflicts with a history of prior mediation by a third party tend to attract additional mediation by that same mediator (Greig, 2005; Regan and Stam, 2000). Solo mediation, however, comes with some important trade-offs. For a weak third party, a solo mediation effort is limited in the resources that can be brought to bear in the talks as a means of pushing the parties to make concessions and leverage an agreement between the two sides. At the same time, because third parties bring their biases with them to the talks, there is little beyond the third party's own restraint to provide balance to these biases in solo mediation.

In multiparty mediation, third parties seek to broker an agreement in the conflict through either several uncoordinated efforts by different third parties, a coalition of third parties working together in a common mediation effort, or sequentially in separate mediation efforts over time (Bohmelt, 2010). Multiparty mediation can sometimes provide a way to overcome some of the limitations of solo mediation. Joining forces with other third parties and engaging in multiparty mediation can provide a means of pooling resources among several actors, giving the third parties more leverage over the conflict and allowing for more effective mediation (Crocker et al., 2001).

Multiparty mediation can also provide a means to balance the biases of the third party providing mediation (Bohmelt,

2010), and thereby give greater legitimacy to the process. For many conflicts, it is much harder for the belligerents to accept mediation from a third party that they see as biased toward the other side. Multiparty mediation can provide a means by which both sides can have a third party at the table that they see as sympathetic to their interests. During the civil war in Tajikistan during the 1990s, both Russia and Iran played important roles mediating the conflict, each joining the talks because they feared that the opposing sides that they supported in the conflict could not win the war (Iji, 2001). As the Russians supported the Tajik government in the conflict, the involvement of Russian mediators in the peace process provided a third party that was seen as trustworthy by the Tajik government. Iranian support for the opposition provided a similar sense of trust in a third party for the rebel side. By including both Iran and Russia in the talks, along with Tajikistan's regional neighbors Uzbekistan, Kazakhstan, Kyrgyzstan, Pakistan, Afghanistan, and Turkmenistan, the mediation process had a balanced coalition of third parties with differing positions on the two sides involved in the conflict, but a shared interest in managing the violence.

Multiparty mediation also comes with some important downsides. Unlike mediation efforts conducted by just one third party, multiparty mediation brings multiple actors into the diplomatic process, each of whom brings their own interests, conflict management approach, and beliefs. Without good coordination among these third parties, multiparty mediation efforts run the risk of confusing a situation even further, making it harder for the two sides to communicate their bargaining positions, capabilities, and commitment to the peace process, prerequisites for an eventual settlement. Two problems of multiparty mediation are its tendencies, if the third parties do not coordinate their actions well, to encourage mixed messages by the mediators on the one hand,

and forum shopping by the belligerents on the other (Crocker et al., 2001). If mediators are not on the same page, they can send different and sometimes contradictory messages to the conflicting sides about the strategies to be used by the third parties during the mediation process, the resources they are willing to bring to bear during the talks, and the goals they have for the mediation effort. In turn, these mixed messages can cause uncertainty and unmet expectations among the two sides, raising the risk that the mediation process will fail as the two sides sour on diplomacy.

The tendency of conflict belligerents to forum shop is also a danger if the mediating coalition does not present a united front during the talks. Similar to parties in a lawsuit searching for the most favorable legal venue, disputants might seek out preferred mediators. This can create chaos in the mediation process, encouraging mixed messages from the mediators as each side tries to raise its own issues with the mediator that it regards as most sympathetic to its position while simultaneously undermining mediator control of the talks. The risks of forum shopping are particularly acute when multiparty mediation occurs through simultaneous and uncoordinated mediation efforts. This problem was especially challenging during the large number mediation efforts directed at the Cambodian Civil War, with the large number of regional powers separately seeking to mediate the conflict, providing substantial opportunities for conflict factions to engage in forum shopping (Solomon, 1999; 2000).

Figure 3.3 compares the occurrence of single and multiparty mediation in conflicts. Among post-World War II mediation attempts, a majority (52%) are conducted by just one mediator. Mediation efforts conducted by states have a greater tendency than those applied by international organizations to involve just one mediator. Whereas 62% of state mediation efforts use just one mediator, only 54% of IO mediation efforts are

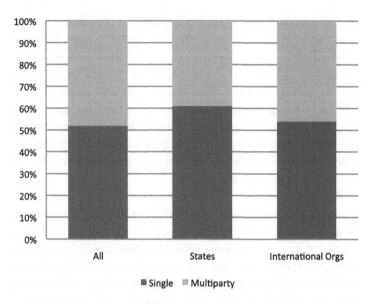

Figure 3.3 Single and Multiparty Mediation

conducted by a single mediator. Among multiparty mediation efforts, an even clearer difference exists between states and IOs in terms of the make-up of the mediation team. When international organizations engage in multiparty mediation, they tend to do so by involving third parties with similar interests. For international organizations, multiparty mediation efforts in which the third parties have different interests in the conflict account for less than 5% of all of their mediation efforts. By contrast, more than 41% of IO mediation efforts are conducted by two or more third parties with similar interests in the conflict.

Multiparty state mediation efforts are much more focused on balancing the positions of the third parties than international organizations, bringing additional third parties into the mediation process in order to balance the biases of the other

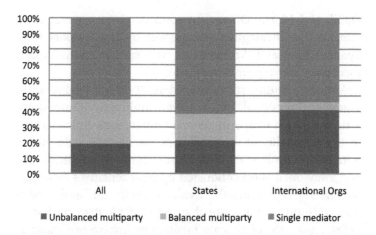

Figure 3.4 Balance of Mediator Interests

third parties. Figure 3.4 describes the balance of mediator interests in single and multiparty mediation efforts. Among state mediation efforts, 21% of all mediation efforts involve two or more third parties holding the same interests in the conflict to be mediated, a proportion that is half that of international organizations. Balanced multiparty state mediation efforts in which the third parties have different interests in the conflict represent about 17% of all state mediation efforts, more than three times greater than that of international organizations. In total, 95% of all cases of IO mediation lack an additional third party with different interests in the conflict whereas less than 83% of state mediation efforts are similarly unbalanced.

Even if a mediation effort is conducted by multiple parties, it need not be drawn from multiple countries. For example, the 1983 mediation effort by the United States aimed at negotiating an agreement between Israel and Lebanon following Israel's 1982 invasion was conducted by American Secretary of State George Shultz and US Middle East envoys Philip

Habib and Morris Draper. In contrast, the 1993 mediation effort of the Nicaraguan Contra War by ambassadors from Spain, Chile, and Argentina is an example of multiparty mediation drawn from several countries.

Although multiparty state mediation efforts tend to show a greater diversity of interests than multiparty IO missions, state mediation efforts in general tend to show little diversity in the nationality of the mediators. An average state mediation effort involves representatives from 1.4 countries. Far and away, mediation conducted by representatives from just one nation represents the modal category for state mediation, accounting for more than 83% of all state mediation cases. About 8% of all state mediations involve two states as third parties. Some of these two-mediator efforts involve third parties with significant differences between them. For example, the United States and Soviet Union jointly mediated the Arab–Israeli Yom Kippur War in 1973 and the Cambodian Civil War in 1991, both of which were significant threats to regional security. The broadest state mediation effort involved ten mediators seeking in 1979 to broker a settlement to the Chad Civil War. This diplomatic intervention involved the combined mediation efforts of all of the states bordering Chad plus Senegal, Benin, Congo, and Liberia.

Multiparty mediation efforts can also occur sequentially in a conflict, with different third parties attempting to settle a conflict at distinct points in time. Among mediated conflicts, the average number of third parties providing mediation during the lifetime of the conflict is 8.8, a seemingly high number. This number, however, is highly skewed. Figure 3.5 charts the number of mediators experienced by conflicts over the lifetime of the conflict. The largest portion of conflicts, 28%, attracts mediation from just one third party. All total, more than half of all mediated conflicts draw three or fewer different mediators to the conflict. The biggest outlier

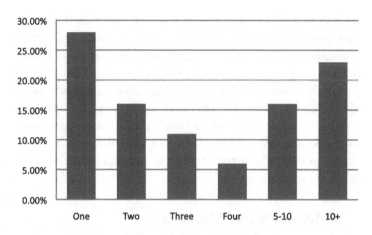

Figure 3.5 Number of Parties Providing Mediation to a Conflict (Lifetime)

among mediated conflicts is the Balkans War in the former Yugoslavia, which saw diplomatic intervention by 144 distinct third parties during the course of the conflict! The Nagorno-Karabakh conflict between Armenia and Azerbaijan and the Sierra Leone Civil War similarly drew many mediation efforts by different third parties, each attracting diplomatic assistance from over fifty distinct third parties. A portion of these cases of different mediators involve some of the original individuals, but these are subsequently joined by others in the third-party lineup. For example, Lord Carrington mediated the Balkan War by himself on several occasions but also mediated the conflict with Portuguese diplomat Jose Cutilero. Many others, however, consist of entirely different collections of third parties.

Looking at the conflicts attracting the largest number of different mediators shows two clear connections among them. Each highly mediated conflict is either a long-running conflict that represents a significant threat to regional security or is a conflict in which major powers have a clear interest at stake. The Sierra Leone Civil War, for example, lasted more than a decade, produced tens of thousands of deaths, and drew military intervention from outside forces. Because of their proximity and shared history, Russia had a strong interest in the conflict between Armenia and Azerbaijan over Nagorno-Karabakh. Many of the most highly mediated conflicts such as the Balkan War and the Lebanese Civil War had a combination of both major-power interest and significant regional security implications.

Motivations for Mediation

The mediation process is a joint decision made by the disputants and the third party. In this section, we focus not on the decision to seek peaceful conflict management per se; this is discussed in the next chapter when we cover getting to the table. Rather we look here at how particular third parties come to be involved in mediation. Mediators might enter a conflict via invitation by the disputants, at their own instigation, or through previous agreements or arrangements with alliances or international organizations. In practice, however, these different pathways are not necessarily distinct. Conflict participants tend to invite third parties that they trust and know will accept or with whom they already have prior relationships. Similarly potential mediators do not travel the globe searching for any conflict to mediate. They target certain conflicts in which they can expect that offers of mediation will be accepted. Thus, deciding on a particular mediator is a collaborative exercise between primary and third parties in which mediator availability and disputant preferences are coordinated. Not surprisingly then, the vast majority of all offers to mediate are accepted, over 92%.

Below, we discuss the most common motives for mediators to get involved in a conflict, focusing on altruistic and self-interested concerns. We also consider the kind of characteristics that conflict parties look for in a mediator and therefore factors that might influence their willingness to accept a given third party.

Mediator Humanitarian Motives
Third-party conflict management efforts to help mitigate and stop an ongoing conflict are often seen as altruistically motivated. A desire to prevent escalation of a conflict, limit its potential for expansion, and promote peace can be important motivating forces for mediation (Bercovitch, 2002). For some diplomatic efforts, such as those motivated by humanitarian concerns, there may be few, if any, direct benefits to the third party providing mediation. Instead, the motivation for providing mediation arises because the third party sees the ongoing conflict and its effects on civilians as creating a humanitarian emergency of sufficient magnitude to require some actor to do something about the conflict. This can even create a situation in which one can plausibly argue that the third party providing mediation actually cares more about the effect of the conflict on the civilian populace than the belligerents themselves, as occurred during conflicts in the Balkans, Sudan, and the Congo (Crocker et al., 2004).

Examining the use of mediation in the face of humanitarian emergencies during the post-World War II period shows some evidence that mediation efforts are at least partially motivated by humanitarian concerns. Figure 3.6 shows the differences in the application of mediation by third-party type to conflicts experiencing genocide. Among all mediation efforts, slightly more than 13% (337 mediations) occur in a conflict in which genocide is occurring. NGOs are the most likely actors to mediate during genocide, directing 22% (twenty-four mediations) of their mediation efforts toward conflicts

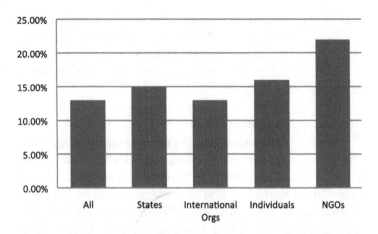

Figure 3.6 Share of Mediation Efforts to Conflicts with Genocide

where genocide is ongoing. For example, during the Second Sudanese Civil War, representatives from the New Sudan Council of Churches provided substantial mediation aimed at managing inter-ethnic fighting in the country. Similarly, the Inter-Religious Council of Sierra Leone played a key role in mediating the country's civil war, providing the foundation for the Lome Peace Agreement between the warring sides (Turay, 2000). Somewhat surprisingly, international organizations, which are commonly seen as attracting the toughest mediation cases that are ignored by the international community, have roughly the same tendency to mediate conflicts experiencing genocide as states do.

States and individuals have relatively similar tendencies toward mediation during genocide, with 15% and 16%, respectively, of their efforts applied to conflicts experiencing genocide. Nevertheless, there is a more marked difference in the share of mediation attention devoted to conflicts with genocide between major and non-major powers. Major powers focus less than 9% their mediation efforts at conflicts accompanied by genocide. By contrast, non-major powers devote more than double the amount of their mediation attention to these conflicts, applying 21% of their mediation work to conflicts experiencing genocide. Many of the conflicts with the worst humanitarian emergencies are ignored by major-power mediators, leaving their mediation to non-major powers and non-state actors, if those conflicts are mediated at all.

At lower levels of humanitarian emergency, refugee crises that occur during a conflict bring a more varied response from the international community. Patterns of mediation involvement in refugee situations are generally similar across actor types, with a few exceptions. Individuals and, to a lesser extent, states show the greatest tendency to send mediators to conflicts producing high levels of refugee flows. Nearly 70% of all mediation efforts by individuals are sent to conflicts with medium to high levels of human displacement, with 28% of individual efforts sent to the conflicts with the largest number of refugees. Among state mediators, more than half of all of their mediations are applied to conflicts producing medium–high levels of refugee flows, with a plurality of state mediations directed at those conflicts that produce the largest number of refugees. This tendency by states to mediate refugee-producing conflicts is consistent with the argument that civilian displacement tends to foster regional instability and undermine economic development (Collier and Hoeffler, 2004; Gleditsch, 2007), creating significant incentives for states to mediate these conflicts.

Mediation efforts motivated simply by a desire to promote peace can, over time, bring benefits to individual states by allowing them to develop international reputations as "good citizens" who are able to stand above realpolitik calculations and step in to bring peace to conflict zones. In this respect, states can sometimes be motivated to offer mediation because it helps to project a positive image of them within the international community. Indeed, some states, notably Norway, have developed a niche as a mediator of conflicts across the international system, despite a lack of clear interests at stake in the conflicts themselves. Norway has been an active mediator between Israel and the PLO and in civil conflicts in Sudan, the former Yugoslavia, and Sri Lanka. Despite a lack of strategic interests in any of these conflicts, Norwegian mediation both helps to support an image of Norway as an important, moral state, an image that resonates in Norwegian public opinion, and carves out a role for the country as a peacemaker in international politics that exceeds what its power position would predict (Hoglund and Svensson, 2009).

Mediator National Interests
Most mediation efforts are motivated by the more direct interests of the third party. For example, among civil conflicts, Greig and Regan (2008) argue that offers of mediation are most directly tied to the interests at stake for the third party in the conflict. During the 1990s Casamance Conflict in Senegal, for example, both Gambia and Guinea-Bissau offered mediation to the government and rebels. Because Gambia and Guinea-Bissau bordered Senegal, the threat of conflict spillover and the push of refugees into their territory provided sufficient interest for their diplomatic involvement in the conflict. Similarly, Algeria's shared borders with Mali provided substantial motivation for its mediation during Mali's Tuareg revolt (Svensson, 2007a). Mediation is best thought of as one among many foreign policy tools available to states to deal with a threat to their interests (Zartman, 2008). Providing mediation to a conflict involves both costs and risks for the third party. Not only do mediators spend time, energy, and resources in attempting to manage a conflict, they also put their reputation at stake by mediating. Actors that

develop a poor track record as mediators risk being seen as weak and ineffective, making them less able to manage other conflicts that may be of even more vital interest to them. As a result, states considering offering mediation must weigh the pros and cons of interventions, gauging the degree to which diplomatic intervention is likely to be an effective means of advancing its foreign policy and domestic political interests (Touval, 2003; Zartman, 2002).

From a foreign policy perspective, mediation can serve as a means of advancing a state's interests by expanding its sphere of influence or defending what is seen as a favorable status quo (Bercovitch, 2002). Soviet mediation between India and Pakistan during the Cold War is a good example of the use of mediation as a means of expanding influence. By acting as intermediary between India and Pakistan, the Soviet Union sought to develop better relations with Pakistan, increasing its role in the region while simultaneously limiting China's (Zartman, 2008).

Mediation is often motivated by a desire to advance multiple interests at the same time. The American role as the key mediator in conflicts in the Middle East is a function of several simultaneous interests. The close relationship between Israel and the United States gives the USA an important interest in Israeli security and has been a key motivation behind its efforts to mediate between it, the Palestinians, and neighboring Arab states. At the same time, the US–Israeli relationship plays an important role in American domestic politics, providing further encouragement for American diplomatic engagement in the Middle East. During the Cold War, American mediation efforts in the Middle East were also driven by defensive aims, motivated by a desire to limit Soviet involvement in the region. US Secretary of State Henry Kissinger, for example, described the 1970 American mediation effort to end the War of Attrition between Israel and Egypt as motivated by a desire to remove Soviet military influence from the region (Touval, 2003).

Smaller states can also have interests that push them toward stepping in and offering mediation. Unlike major powers, they are likely to have fewer foreign policy tools at their disposal to effect change in a conflict. As a result, a smaller state that wants to protect interests that are threatened by an ongoing conflict may see no other choice but to mediate an end to the fighting (Zartman, 2008). During the early 1990s civil conflict in Tajikistan, both neighboring Kazakhstan and Turkmenistan helped mediate the conflict with Russia and Iran. Unlike Russia and Iran, which each supported different sides in the conflict, participation in the mediation by Kazakhstan and Turkmenistan was primarily driven by their shared fear that the Tajik conflict could spill across the border and threaten their own security (Iji, 2001).

Algerian mediation in 1980 between the United States and Iran during the hostage crisis is an example of a small state providing mediation as a means of expanding its influence beyond that which its power position would normally command. Because Algeria had close links to both Iran and the United States and was viewed as trustworthy by both sides, it was singularly well positioned to act as a mediator among the two sides. Algeria was significantly weaker than the two sides that it mediated during the hostage crisis, and therefore it lacked the resources to leverage concessions from the two sides or to provide them with incentives for agreement. Algeria, however, did provide what the two sides otherwise lacked, a means to communicate with one another. Given that diplomatic relations between the USA and Iran were cut off following the Iranian Revolution and the seizing of the US embassy in Tehran, Algeria was the most effective conduit for negotiations between the two sides, negotiations that ultimately provided the framework

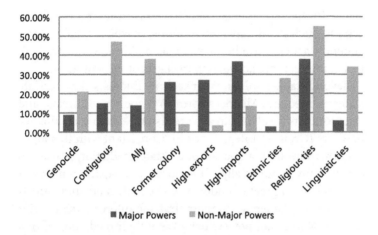

Figure 3.7   State Interests and Mediation

for the release of the US hostages and the creation of the Iran–US Claims Tribunal.

In examining the post-World War II mediation record, we see clear signs that state interests play an important role in influencing where states mediate. The impact of these interests on the use mediation by states is described in Figure 3.7. About 31% of all state mediation efforts are directed at conflicts involving a neighboring state, suggesting that states pay a significant amount of their attention to those conflicts that are likely to have the most direct impact upon their own security and interests. There are some important differences in the use of mediation by major and non-major power states. Major powers, because they tend to have broader and more diverse interests than other states and are often located in more stable regions, only direct about 15% of their mediation efforts at conflicts in neighboring states. Non-major powers are more likely to focus their mediation attention closer to home, using 47% of their mediation efforts in conflicts involving neighboring states. In this way, mediation behavior mirrors more coercive actions, such as military interventions, in which smaller states generally act closer to home whereas major power states with global interests are active in many parts of the world.

Beyond stable borders, other security interests also motivate states to mediate. Alliances form in response to threats, and thus conflicts involving an ally are also threats to their alliance partners (Greig and Regan, 2008). Consistent with this logic, slightly more than a quarter of all state mediation is used in conflicts involving an ally of the third party. Again, non-major powers show a greater tendency to use their mediation efforts to deal with challenges to their strategic interests than major powers. Non-major powers use 38% of their mediation efforts in conflicts involving a state allied to them. Major powers use a much smaller fraction of their activity in conflicts involving their allies, applying about 14% of their mediation efforts to their alliance partners. These differences in mediation behavior toward allies are most likely rooted in an important difference between major and non-major powers. Confronted with a threat to their allies, major power states have a variety of tools beyond mediation including direct intervention, financial aid, and military assistance available to deal with the threat. Because of their more limited capabilities, non-major powers often have fewer policy options open to them to deal with such a threat, leaving mediation as their best means of dealing with the challenge.

Bilateral trade ties are also an important interest for states. High levels of bilateral trade, for example, increase the likelihood of outside intervention in international conflicts (Regan and Aydin, 2006). Along these same lines, although major powers use mediation in conflicts involving their allies and neighbors less frequently than non-major powers, they tend to focus their diplomatic efforts on conflicts involving important trade partners to a greater degree than non-major powers. Among major powers, nearly 38% of their mediation efforts are devoted to conflicts involving trade partners in the top quartile of exports to the third party. France, for example, mediated between two former colonies, Morocco, a key trading partner, and Mauritania, during the Western Sahara Conflict. Non-major powers, by contrast, only use about 14% of their mediation efforts for conflict states with the largest amount of exports to them. Part of this finding is no doubt a selection effect, with non-major powers tending to import a smaller total amount of goods from most countries than major powers. At the same time, this difference in mediation behavior suggests that non-major powers may concentrate their diplomatic energies on conflicts that are more direct security threats to them, such as conflicts involving allies and neighbors, rather than less vital threats to trade partners.

Beyond these strategic interests that inspire mediation by states, the willingness of states to offer mediation is also influenced by their broader linkages with the parties involved in the conflict. Although some of these interests may rise to the level of national security interests, others, such as economic and social linkages, retain sufficient importance to encourage an offer of mediation to the conflict. Social links, economic ties, and security interests between Egypt and Yemen, for example, encouraged Egyptian mediation efforts during Yemen's civil war during the 1990s. In this respect, not only do alliance linkages between a belligerent and a third party tend to encourage an offer of mediation, but trade ties between the two also increase the propensity for mediation (Crescenzi et al., 2011). Historical linkages, such as a prior colonial relationship or shared ethnic and religious ties between an outside side and the civil war parties, also tend to foster mediation (Greig, 2005; Greig and Regan, 2008). Iran became involved in the Tajikistan civil war and offered assistance as a mediator, for example, because it not only shares a border with Tajikistan, but also significant linguistic, cultural, and historical ties (Iji, 2001).

Mediation by major powers such France and Britain in their former colonies is common, but the historical linkages between smaller states and their former colonies have also encouraged their willingness to offer mediation. Belgium, for example, has maintained an active conflict management role in its former colonies in the Great Lakes region of Africa. This conflict management role for Belgium is a function of what the former colonial power sees as its continuing responsibility to its former colonies and the region. In 2003, Koen Vervaeke, Belgian Special Envoy for the Great Lakes Region, described this responsibility as:

> Strictly spoken, Belgium no longer has any vital interests to protect in Central Africa, even in the Democratic Republic of Congo, despite its potential riches. But Belgium is convinced that it has a moral responsibility to demonstrate solidarity with the region in Africa it knows best and where it still has numerous ties ... (T)here is a strong feeling that we owe these countries something.
>
> (Vervaeke, 2003: 1–2)

Mediation efforts by former colonial powers account for about 15% of all cases of state mediation. Not surprisingly, major powers, states with the most extensive number of former colonies, devote more than seven times the share of their mediation activity to their former colonies than non-major powers; for major powers, mediation in their former colonies represents nearly 26% of their total mediation activity. Among non-major powers, Portugal is the most active mediator in its former colonies, mediating frequently during the conflict between South Africa and its former colony Angola over Namibia. In 1998, Portugal also mediated during the civil war in Guinea-Bissau, a colonial possession that became independent in 1974.

Colonial ties can create a shared historical bond between colonizer and former colony, but shared ethnic linkages, a common language, and religious ties (these frequently overlap and are reinforcing influences) are social connections that can provide an interest for a third party to mediate a conflict as well. Among post-World War II conflicts, social linkages represent a significantly stronger influence on non-major power mediation behavior than major power behavior. For example, just less than 28% of all non-major power mediation efforts are directed at disputants that share the same majority ethnic group as the third-party state. Linguistic connections between non-major power mediators and conflict participants are even stronger, with nearly 34% of all non-major power mediation efforts being applied to conflicts in which at least one of the state participants shares the same majority religious group as the mediator. Religious ties between non-major powers and conflict participants represent an even stronger influence, linking nearly 55% of all non-major power mediation efforts. During the Second Lebanese Civil War, Iran, Algeria, and Syria all played active roles in mediating the conflict. Beyond their strategic interests that encouraged involvement in the conflict, each of these third parties also held important religious ties to participants in the conflict.

The effect of social connections on major power mediation activity is considerably weaker. Less than 3% of major power mediation efforts are sent to conflicts in which a shared ethnic tie is present. Linguistic connections are more strongly linked to major power mediation, but still constitute only 6% of all major power mediation efforts. Only religious connections constitute a significant tie for major power mediation, comprising 38% of all major power diplomatic interventions. This effect is still markedly smaller than the connection between religious ties and non-major power mediation. The ethnic, religious, and linguistic ties between the United States and the United Kingdom provided some of the American interest in mediating the Falklands War between Argentina and the United Kingdom, although it is difficult to disentangle these interests from the broader strategic goals of major powers. A similar set of ties encouraged Jordanian efforts to mediate following the Iraqi invasion of Kuwait in 1990, although even here the use of mediation is driven by wider strategic interests.

Mediator Organizational Interests

International organizations also have interests that motivate them to provide mediation to some ongoing conflicts. Many international organizations have the maintenance of peace and security specified as their core goal. Some may even have a specific mandate for intervention in conflicts among their member states (Bercovitch, 2002). A desire to establish a conflict management role and peacemaking reputation for itself can be the impetus for an international organization to mediate a conflict (Zartman, 2008). International organizations sometimes wind up mediating conflicts because no one else is willing to do so. These "wards of the system" are conflicts such as the civil wars in Somalia, Rwanda, and Mozambique that are largely ignored by states and left to IOs to manage (Crocker et al., 2004).

At the same time, because international organizations are created by and act at the behest of their member states, their interests are a function of the interests of their member states. Regional organizations, such as the African Union, OAS, or Arab League, mediate conflicts when their members see it as in their interests for mediation to occur (Zartman, 2002). Which interests matter in determining whether mediation is used depends substantially on the governing structure of the international organization, the distribution of power among member states, and the level of variation in their interests in and aims for a specific conflict. In the United Nations, because of the important role that the Security Council plays in dealing with global conflicts, members of the Security Council, especially the veto-wielding permanent members, exert significant influence over where and when mediation efforts are used. Within regional organizations like the African Union, regional powers like Nigeria and South Africa exert significant influence over how the organization deals with conflicts on the African continent.

Disputant Preferences
We know considerably less about disputant choices of particular mediators than we do about what motivates those third parties to become involved. Nevertheless, prior research has focused on the characteristics of ideal mediators from the perspective of the primary parties to the conflict (for a review and extension see Bercovitch and Schneider, 2000). These can roughly be divided according to the characteristics of the actor carrying out the mediation (e.g. states, international organizations) as well as the particular person(s) or agent(s) of the actor who actually conducts the mediation.

At the actor level, as might be expected, disputants desire a mediator that is perceived to be "even-handed," that is willing to broker an agreement fairly (Kaufman and Duncan, 1992). This might come from the neutrality of the mediator, but it is not essential, as we noted above, in that many mediators have their own interests and might be allied with one of the rivals; still, such bias does not necessarily preclude assuming a fair third-party role. Indeed, another desirable trait is the "leverage" that a mediator might bring to the table. In this context, leverage signifies resources and other sources of influence that can facilitate a favorable outcome. It might be noted that a neutral or unbiased mediator might not have as much leverage as a biased one, in that the latter has the potential to persuade a reluctant ally to accept an agreement (Touval and Zartman, 1985a). Given the desirability of mediators with leverage, there is the apparent anomaly of selecting weak mediators who lack such an attribute. Beardsley (2009) argues that weak mediators are more likely when one or more of the combatants wants to use mediation insincerely, that is when the goal is not necessarily to reach an agreement. An insincere disputant might wish to delay the process, face strong domestic/constituency pressures to resist concessions, or recognize that bargaining power is shifting. Weak mediators and their likely failure then serve the interests of those who do not want a settlement under the present conditions.

Warring parties might also prefer mediators (especially when states mediate) who come from similar ideological or cultural positions as they do. There is often greater confidence in such actors as well as the purported advantage that they have a better understanding of the disputants and their needs, negotiating styles, and so on than mediators sharing fewer commonalities.

Mediation is actually carried out not by states or organizations per se, but by their chosen individual agents. Although the characteristics of the actor are probably more important than the individual representing the actor, there are nonetheless some clear preferences for certain agent attributes. The most notable might be the legitimacy of the agent, usually reflected in the rank or position of the individual. Disputants desire individuals who are heads of state or have international stature rather than lower-level bureaucratic functionaries. High-ranking individuals appointed as mediators send a signal that the actor takes the conflict seriously and might be more willing to expend effort and resources to facilitate a settlement. Beyond legitimacy, there is a predictable list of agent characteristics that are favored by disputants and indeed reflect the attributes of good diplomats in general; these include being knowledgeable, patient, and having a sense of humor, among others.

In the next two sections, we examine the use of mediation in two long-running, intractable conflicts, each of which draws sustained mediation efforts from the international community. In the Burundian Civil War case, sustained mediation efforts tend to be spearheaded by one individual mediator but are supported by several outside actors. In the Israeli–Palestinian case, we see greater diversity in the providers of mediation and the approaches each takes to managing the conflict.

Mediation in the Burundian Civil War

Mediation of Burundi's 1994–2005 civil war is a good example of the use of sequential, multiparty mediation that assisted warring parties down the long road toward peace. This mediation process was led by three different individuals, former Tanzanian President Julius Nyerere, South African President Nelson Mandela, and South African Deputy President Jacob Zuma. Each brought a different background and approach to the role of mediator, but their cumulative efforts played a decisive role in ending one of the most intractable conflicts of the late twentieth century.

The 1994–2005 Burundian Civil War was among the deadliest and most challenging conflicts to manage during the post-World War II era. The war killed an estimated 300,000 people, internally displaced about 800,000 Burundians, and forced approximately 500,000 civilians to flee across Burundi's borders to neighboring countries (Falch, 2009). The conflict was a continuation of a long-running post-colonial struggle between Burundi's majority Hutus and its Tutsi governing elite, a struggle that had manifested itself into three earlier periods of civil war. The 1994 conflict was touched off by the assassinations of Burundi's newly elected president, Melchior Ndadaye, a Hutu, and members of his Hutu Front for Democracy in Burundi (FRODEBU) political party in October 1993 by Burundi's Tutsi-controlled army in an effort to preserve Tutsi political power (Ngaruko and Nkurunziza, 2005). These assassinations touched off large-scale ethnic violence as Hutus began attacking Tutsi civilians in retaliation for Ndadaye's death and the Tutsi-led military mounted attacks against Hutus. By the summer of 1994, Burundi had descended into a full-scale civil war with multiple armed Hutu opposition groups fighting the Tutsi-led Burundian army. Among these Hutu opposition groups, the two most powerful and important groups were the National Council for the Defense of Democracy-Forces for the Defense of Democracy (CNDD-FDD) and Palipehutu-National Forces of Liberation (FNL), each of which had political and military wings.

Efforts to manage the Burundian Civil War faced a number of significant challenges that made finding an acceptable mediator, getting all of the warring parties to the bargaining table, and achieving and implementing a settlement difficult. Foremost among these challenges were the deep roots of the Burundian conflict, which created a legacy of violence and suspicion among the warring parties that took years of sustained conflict management efforts by multiple parties to overcome. Nguruko and Nkurunziza (2005) describe three root causes of Burundi's civil conflict. First, during its colonial rule, Belgium promoted a "divide and conquer" policy that encouraged divisions between Hutus and Tutsis. Under this policy, for example, Belgian colonial rulers replaced Hutu chiefs with Tutsis, sharpening the ethnic divide between the two sides. Second, not only was Burundi governed by the minority Tutsis, but the elite was disproportionately drawn from the province of Bururi and adopted policies that advantaged that region and further fractured Burundian society.

Finally, the experience of the 1959 Social Revolution in neighboring Rwanda, which shifted power from Rwanda's Tutsis to the majority Hutus, served to encourage similar ambitions for Burundi's Hutus while also providing a vivid example to Burundi's Tutsis about the consequences of majority rule in their country. In this respect, mediating the Burundian Civil War was not simply an effort at managing a contemporary conflict, but was also one that required dealing with a legacy of historic grievances and fears between multiple groups in Burundi.

In 1996, nearly two years into the Burundian Civil War, Former Tanzanian President Julius Nyerere stepped in as mediator. Nyerere's selection as mediator of the conflict was influenced by parties both internal and external to the conflict. Because of his international prominence and familiarity with the conflict, Nyerere was recommended by the Carter Center and requested by Presidents Mandela of South Africa, Musevani of Uganda, and Zenawi of Ethiopia, and was seen as the only third party capable of gaining the trust of all groups in the conflict (Bentley and Southall, 2005). Nyerere's international reputation was shaped by the key role that he played in the establishment of the Organization of African Unity, Tanzania's defeat of Idi Amin's Uganda during this presidency, and his long history of support for the anti-apartheid movement in South Africa. Nyerere also had extensive involvement in Burundian politics dating from the 1960s where he supported demands for majority Hutu rule. Although this prior experience in Burundian politics gave Nyerere extensive knowledge of Burundi, its conflict, and the participants in the conflict, it also raised questions about his neutrality and trustworthiness for some parties to the conflict. Tutsi groups in Burundi, because of his prior support for Hutu rule, viewed mediation by Nyerere skeptically (Bentley and Southall, 2005).

A key feature of Nyerere's mediation in Burundi was that, while the effort was conducted by a private individual, Nyerere worked closely with regional African leaders and key outside powers such as the USA, France, Belgium, the UN, and the EU. Initial talks began in April 1996 and brought together the key Tutsi political group, the Union for National Progress (UPRONA), and the FRODEBU. Shortly thereafter, regional African state leaders called a summit in Arusha, Tanzania to discuss the conflict in Burundi and push the sides to accept a peacekeeping force to stabilize the situation. Fearing the consequences of a peacekeeping force, the Burundian army launched a coup and installed former President Pierre Buyoya in power. In response, regional states imposed a blockade on Burundi, a step that Nyerere saw as useful in increasing pressure on the Tutsi-led government without the complications to the peace process that a military intervention by regional powers would bring (Bentley and Southall, 2005).

Nyerere's mediation efforts continued throughout 1996 and 1997, but were stymied by the refusal of the Burundi government to attend the talks or to permit any groups in Burundi to do so. Ultimately, a second round of talks mediated by Nyerere and hosted by the government of Tanzania were held in June 1998 in which nineteen delegations from Burundi participated as well as the leaders of regional states Kenya, Uganda, Rwanda, Ethiopia, and Zaire. These talks, however, made little substantive progress as the Burundian government refused to make the concessions demanded by the regional powers, which in turn refused to lift their economic sanctions. Nevertheless, simply bringing the large number of conflict parties to the bargaining table was an important initial step toward the eventual agreement that would follow.

Following Nyerere's death in 1999, South African President Nelson Mandela took over as mediator of the conflict. Similar to Nyerere, Mandela enjoyed substantial international stature and was effective in using that support as leverage during the talks. In particular, Mandela was able to mobilize resources for Burundi from both the EU and the USA and actually brought the leaders of Saudi Arabia, France, the United States, and Nigeria into a session of the talks. The transition from Nyerere to Mandela illustrates the important role that the individual characteristics of the mediator and the differences in their mediation strategies play in shaping the conduct of a conflict management effort, topics that are raised in the following chapter.

Whereas Nyerere was seen by Tutsis as too closely tied to the Tanzanian government, Mandela was seen as more even-handed between the warring sides and more skeptical of the interests of Burundi's regional neighbors largely because of his role in South Africa's post-apartheid reconciliation (Bentley and Southall, 2005). Although both Nyerere and Mandela sought to make the talks that they brokered broadly inclusive, there were important differences in which parties each sought to include in the talks. For Nyerere, military action against governments was seen as illegal. As a result, he refused to include the rebel leaders in the talks (Bentley and Southall, 2005). Some have argued that Nyerere's decision to exclude rebel leaders from the talks had less to do with the legality of the use of armed force against a government and more to do with a desire to maintain military pressure on the Burundian government to encourage movement in the talks (Mthembu-Salter, 2002). Because of his own experience with the African National Congress during South Africa's apartheid era, Mandela emphasized the importance of including the leaders of rebel groups in the talks alongside the leaders of Burundi's political parties (Bentley and Southall, 2005; Reyntjens, 2005).

Over time, Mandela's mediation effort began to pay off. In order to create pressure for an agreement and motivate progress on the talks, Mandela set a deadline for agreement. The Arusha

Accord was reached among most of the delegations in August 2000, but several Tutsi groups refused to sign the agreement. The agreement established a three-year implementation period in which then-President Buyoya, a Tutsi, would maintain power for eighteen months before it was transitioned to Hutu and FRODEBU leader Domitien Ndayizeye for a subsequent eighteen-month period. As a consequence of the holdouts to the Arusha Accords, both diplomacy and conflict continued over the next several years, with South African Deputy President Jacob Zuma stepping in as mediator after Mandela left office. In April 2003, presidential power in Burundi was successfully transferred as Buyoya stepped down and Ndayizeye took office. In October 2003, mediation by Zuma produced the Protocol on Political Power-Sharing, Defense, and Security, with a full power-sharing agreement signed in August 2004. An interim constitution was approved by the parliament in October 2004 and ratified by voters in early 2005.

The Burundi mediation was technically carried out by non-governmental officials who had substantial altruistic motives to manage the conflict. Both Nyerere and Mandela had strong commitments to African peace and stability. Yet these distinguished statesmen were also backed by the Organization of African Unity and surrounding states that had clear strategic interests in solving the Burundi conflict. The specter of another genocide on the scale of Rwanda – note that Burundi has the same two opposing ethnic groups – was strong incentive for the international community to act, as were the refugee flows and negative externalities present for surrounding states.

Mediating the Israeli–Palestinian Conflict

Efforts to mediate the Israeli–Palestinian conflict faced a set of challenges that are both similar to and distinct from those present in the Burundian Civil War. As with the conflict in Burundi, the Israeli–Palestinian conflict is a long-running, intractable conflict in which each of the contending sides feels victimized by the other and a substantial legacy of fear and mistrust among the parties has developed. Just as the Burundian Civil War was enmeshed in the other conflicts of Africa's Great Lakes Region, the Israeli–Palestinian conflict has been closely linked to the wider conflicts between Israel and neighboring Arab states. At the same time, there are some important differences between the two conflicts. Whereas the Burundian conflict is a civil war that has drawn the interest of international actors, the Israeli–Palestinian conflict is neither purely a civil war nor an interstate conflict, creating unique difficulties for third parties seeking to mediate it. The Burundian conflict involved a multitude of political and military actors, requiring representatives of more than twenty different groups to sit down at the bargaining table during talks. The number of important actors in the Israeli–Palestinian conflict is smaller, but the players on the two sides are no more cohesive. The Palestinian side is divided between Fatah and Hamas factions, each with distinct political leaders, positions toward Israel, and policy objectives. Third parties mediating the Israeli–Palestinian conflict must also deal with the divisions on the Israeli side. Changes in the political party governing Israel have historically had an important impact on talks between the Israelis and Palestinians.

The Israeli–Palestinian conflict is rooted in the 1948 establishment of the state of Israel. Immediately after its establishment, Israel's regional neighbors declared war on the new state, fighting a series of losing conflicts with it that resulted in the expansion of Israel's territorial holdings. Following the 1967 Six Day War, Israel captured the Sinai Peninsula and Gaza Strip from Egypt, the West Bank from Jordan, and the Golan Heights from Syria. Over the decades, mediation efforts between Israelis and Palestinians have focused on dealing with the four core and somewhat interrelated issues between the Israelis and Palestinians: control over Jerusalem, the status of Palestinian refugees displaced during the establishment of Israel and in the subsequent wars, the final borders and security arrangements between Israel and a Palestinian state, and the disposition of Israeli settlements in the West Bank. These mediation efforts have shown periods of fits and starts, with moments of optimism often followed by the collapse of peace initiatives and renewed pessimism.

Mediation between the Israelis and Palestinians has been conducted by multiple third parties but has been less systematically coordinated than the efforts by Nyerere and Mandela in Burundi. The United States has played the most active role in mediating between the Israelis and Palestinians over the years, but other actors have also played important roles as well. During 1985–1986, Jordan's King Hussein worked with US Secretary of State George Shultz to attempt to mediate between Israel and the Palestinians, although little progress was made between the two sides. The 1991 Madrid Conference sponsored by the United States and the Soviet Union represented a broad effort to bring the Palestinians and Israelis together at the negotiating table along with Jordan, Lebanon, and Syria. Although these talks ultimately stalled, they nonetheless were the first effort in which indirect talks took place between Israel and the PLO. This alone was an important step as Israel had historically refused to negotiate with the PLO, which it saw as a terrorist group that refused to recognize Israel's right to exist. The 1985 Hussein–Shultz mediation sought to circumvent Israeli unwillingness to deal directly with the PLO by including Palestinian representatives chosen by the PLO in the Jordanian negotiating delegation, a path that was subsequently followed during the Madrid Conference.

Other states have played a more informal role in mediating between Israel and the Palestinians. In 1992, Egyptian Foreign Minister Amr Moussa served as a go-between, transmitting questions and answers between the head of the PLO's Department for National and International Relations and the Israeli Prime Minister and Foreign Minister (Kriesberg, 2001). At various points in time, Jordan has also served as an informal go-between between the two sides. The 1993 Norwegian effort that cumulated with the Oslo Accords began with back-channel talks between informal representatives of the two sides, developing into a much more extensive peace process that ultimately yielded the September 1993 statement of joint recognition by the Israeli and Palestinian sides and the Declaration of Principles Agreement. Although the parties failed to seize the momentum produced at Oslo, the talks did establish limited Palestinian self-government and attempted to lay the groundwork for permanent status negotiations over the core issues in dispute.

American mediation efforts directed at the Israeli–Palestinian conflict resemble more traditional, power-based mediation than the more informal talks during the Oslo peace process. The Norwegian-sponsored Oslo talks emphasized the importance of building a personal rapport between the individual representatives of the two sides as a means of overcoming the enemy images held by each side (Schulz, 2004). In contrast, American mediation efforts toward the conflict have tended to be more top-down in focus, seeking to use both carrots and sticks to leverage the parties toward an agreement, an approach that was well suited to the unique American capacity to bring substantial resources to bear to the talks and its strong commitment to managing the conflict (Kriesberg, 2001). American mediation efforts during the 1998 Wye River talks, which sought to build upon the progress at Oslo and implement the 1995 Interim Agreement between Israel and the Palestinians that established the Palestinian Authority, are a good example of the use of American leverage during its mediation efforts in the conflict. In order to facilitate an agreement during the Wye talks, US President Bill Clinton committed to monitor each side's compliance with an agreement and promised increased economic aid to both Israel and the Palestinians, conditional on their compliance with any agreement reached (Lasensky, 2002). In this respect, the history of mediation between Israel and the Palestinians has seen a diversity of approaches by a number of actors, ranging from strategies that focus on improving communications between the two sides and building trust among them to providing inducements for agreements and offering mechanisms to reassure the two sides that the other will not defect from a settlement.

Mediation in the Israeli–Palestinian conflict involved several different actor types with different motivations. Major powers, such as the United States, had clear strategic interests in resolving the conflict, lest any of the frequent clashes escalate to another war; this concern was especially salient during the Cold War when the Middle East conflict was a handful of "proxy" conflicts with the superpowers. Neighboring states, predominantly Arab, were not seen by Israel as trustworthy enough to play the role of mediator, even as they have strong interests in the conflict. In several ways, their positions as virtual primary parties in the struggle preclude their assumption of third-party roles. Only after making peace with Israel were both Jordan and Egypt able to act as intermediaries in the conflict. Similarly, the perceived or real bias of the UN and the League of Arab States made mediation all but impossible for those two international organizations, even as the former was an important supplier of peacekeeping operations to the region. Finally, states such as Norway and Romania had few vested interests in the conflict, but nonetheless were an important part of the processes that facilitated some limited agreements.

Despite the frequent efforts by a multitude of third parties to mediate the Israeli–Palestinian conflict, the core issues in dispute remain unsettled at the time of writing this, and even the implementation of existing agreements has been slow. The challenges in managing these issues underscores the importance of the motivations and bargaining positions of the contending sides in shaping the effectiveness of third-party diplomacy. Although a third party may have sufficient interest to attempt mediation of a conflict, without the willingness of the two sides to make the concessions necessary to reach an agreement and the will to follow through and implement the agreement, settlement of a conflict will be impossible. In the next chapter, we examine the conditions under which parties in conflict become more willing to make the hard choices necessary to transition from conflict toward peace.

CHAPTER FOUR

The Success and Failure of Mediation

One of the challenges in both the practice and study of mediation is distinguishing between its success and failure. For some cases, identifying success is easy. The Camp David talks that established the lasting peace between Israel and Egypt are a noteworthy example of successful mediation. Yet, examining more deeply how mediated settlements unfold and are implemented raises important questions that make determining success and failure more difficult than appears at first glance. The Camp David talks were a long process that proceeded in fits and starts, with progress at some points and negotiation roadblocks at other points. Once Israel and Egypt signed the Camp David Accords in 1978, one could certainly describe the outcome as a success, and the durable peace between two former enemies is consistent with labeling the mediation effort successful, even if the peace is not "positive" (which encompasses harmonious relations and some interdependence). What if Egypt and Israel and had gone to war again in ten years, or five years, or one year? Would the Camp David Accords still be regarded as a "success?" Had a new war happened between the two sides, at least they had reached an agreement with each formally recognizing the other and experienced some interval of reduced hostility, significant steps in their relationship.

Distinguishing success from failure is especially difficult when a mediation effort produces a cease-fire without achieving a lasting settlement to the conflict. This is not

unusual. In our data, slightly more than 10% of all mediation efforts resulted in a cease-fire between the parties, with
the rate of cease-fires being approximately equal in civil and
interstate conflicts. A mediation effort that fosters a cease-
fire between the two sides certainly contributes to peace,
even if for only a short time. Because a mediated cease-fire,
at least temporarily, lessens the level of conflict between
warring sides, it makes sense to label such an achievement
as successful. Long-running cease-fires exist in the conflicts on Cyrus between Greek and Turkish Cypriots, on
the Korean peninsula between North and South Korea, and
among Israel and Syria, each without the establishment of a
permanent peace agreement. Yet some conflicts experience
a revolving door of mediated cease-fires, each subsequently
broken, some lasting for as little as a few hours. The war
in the former Yugoslavia experienced forty-six separate
mediated cease-fires during the course of the conflict. The
Second Lebanese Civil War saw twenty-eight different mediated cease-fires from 1975 to 1992. Although each cease-fire
represents at least a minimal contribution toward conflict
management, as cease-fires increasingly break down repeatedly it becomes more difficult to label their achievement as
"successful."

Just as all cease-fires are not created equally, neither are all
mediation failures. A mediation effort in which no cease-fire
or agreement is reached and the two sides return to fight it
out on the battlefield until one subdues the other is certainly
a failure. Other "failed" mediation efforts, however, may yet
contribute to peace in the long term by exposing the two sides
to new information about one another, improving their ability
to understand each other's positions, and beginning to challenge the adversarial images each has of the other (Princen,
1992; Stein, 1996). Even failed mediation efforts, by bringing the two sides together for face-to-face talks, can begin to

help build trust and a rapport between them that make future mediation more likely to happen and improve the prospects for success of those subsequent mediation efforts (Rubin, 1992; Kelman, 1997; Lederach, 1997; Bercovitch and Gartner, 2006). During the Liberian Civil War, efforts by ECOWAS leaders to mediate the conflict failed in 1990 and only achieved a partial agreement in 1991, to reach more comprehensive settlements in 1996 and 1997.

Thus, for some cases of mediation, there is not a clear delineation between "success" and "failure." Instead, determining the success and failure of a mediation effort depends significantly upon the time horizon of the conflict being examined and the contribution the mediation effort plays in positively improving the relationship between two sides in conflict. Although this can sometimes be hard to identify clearly for some instances of mediation, for many others the divide between success and failure is clearer. Here we focus primarily on success defined in two ways and corresponding to the different stages of the mediation process. The first is the achievement of getting the disputing parties to accept mediation, referred to as "getting to the table." The second is success in the second stage, namely having the parties reach some type of agreement as a result of the mediation; such agreement can vary widely in terms of scope from a simple cease-fire to a comprehensive settlement of all outstanding grievances. These two stages are partly linked in the sense that some of the same factors and processes that encourage actors to seek mediation also influence their willingness to come to an agreement; nevertheless, the two stages are not identical and for analytical purposes we cover them separately below. The third stage of mediation, dealing with implementation concerns and the durability of settlements, is addressed in Chapter 5.

Getting to the Table

The first step in managing a conflict, while no guarantee of ultimate success, is bringing the parties to the bargaining table. Getting the parties to agree to sit down and negotiate provides an opportunity for them to reevaluate their perceptions of the other side, gather new information about the prospects for settlement of the conflict, and communicate information about their own bargaining positions to the other side. Yet, achieving success in this initial stage is often difficult. Because of the "bargainer's dilemma," parties in conflict fear the possibility that peace overtures directed at the other side will be perceived as a sign of weakness that can be exploited. At the same time, disputants also dread the potential domestic political costs from their constituents in sitting down with the enemy, worrying that they might be labeled as appeasers of the enemy or traitors to the cause (Spector, 1998). Nevertheless, when actors perceive that concessions in bargaining might be necessary, mediation can provide the political cover necessary rather than having to give up some demands unilaterally (Beardsley, 2010).

For the most deeply rooted, intractable conflicts, getting the disputants to the bargaining table requires a shift in their expectations about the best way for their conflict to be handled (Stein, 1989). The willingness of parties to negotiate with one another and accept mediation can develop as the costs of conflict between the two sides mount ("pain") and diplomatic approaches to settle the conflict grow more appealing than continued violence ("promise"). That is, mediation is not necessarily the first method of addressing the conflict by the parties. The conflict must be serious enough (often involving some costs) before mediation becomes a desirable option. Furthermore, given that mediators become involved, it means that the parties are unwilling to negotiate directly or have tried to do so unsuccessfully. Overall, there must be some "softening up" before mediation is an attractive alternative to disputatious behavior (Greig and Diehl, 2006). In addition, there are several other factors that influence the willingness of parties to negotiate with one another, including their past relationships and domestic political environment.

Pain

Actors are more likely to pursue mediation when their dispute is especially painful. The pain is most likely to arise from past militarized confrontations, both ongoing and those throughout their history of interaction. Ongoing militarized clashes and wars impose immediate costs on the rivals as well as significant risks that may attend to the escalation of violence. Under these conditions, they may seek alternatives to lessen risks and costs, and therefore negotiations or third-party mediations become more attractive alternatives. During the Korean War, for example, both sides grew more interested in talks as events on the battlefield increasingly signaled the inability of either side to overcome the other (Holsti, 1966). Yet we know that disputants are not myopic and therefore do not make decisions solely on immediate circumstances, but take into account the history of their conflictual interactions as a whole (Goertz et al., 2005). Thus, accumulated costs, evidenced by the severity of past confrontations, might also influence propensity to seek diplomatic alternatives.

A simple cost conception is not necessarily sufficient to bring enemies to the bargaining table and hence a more sophisticated notion is that of "mutually hurting stalemate" or MHS, which is a perceptual condition "in which neither side can win, yet continuing conflict will be very harmful to each" (Zartman, 2003). The existence of this condition is supposed to facilitate disputants coming to the negotiating table and possibly reaching a settlement to their conflict. For example, in mediating between Egypt and Israel during the 1973 October War Henry Kissinger recognized that only a war with neither victory nor defeat could lay the groundwork for settlement and sought to manipulate events to foster this stalemate (Richter, 1992).

MHS has three essential components. The first, "stalemate," signifies an impasse in the conflict such that no party can envision achieving its goals through continued fighting. Zartman (2001: 8) speaks of this as a "plateau" in the relationship ("a flat and unending terrain without relief") and others (Brahm, 2003) characterize it as an apex between escalation and deescalation. The second element, "hurting," signifies that the parties are paying certain costs, with the assumption that these are significant enough to consider changing behavior or direction in the relationship. Although such costs are normally thought of as ongoing, Zartman (2003; 2007b) modifies this consideration somewhat and indicates that an impending, past, or recently avoided catastrophe can serve the same perceptual function as ongoing costs; such a catastrophe can signal to the parties the pain likely to be endured from continuing on the same course of action. The final element, "mutually," indicates that each party is experiencing significant costs and has little chance of succeeding through continued coercion. A one-sided hurting stalemate would leave a situation in which the unconstrained side may continue fighting and reject any settlement attempts. Although the pain must be mutual, it does not necessarily have to be equal or from the same sources (Zartman, 2001; 2007a). The implication is that there must be some minimum level of costs for all sides, but without regard to whether all parties are paying similar costs. Zartman (2000), for example, argues that it was not until the FMLN rebels in El Salvador launched their offensive against major cities that both sides realized that the costs of conflict were high and conflict was unlikely to change the status quo. He points out that the offensive served to convince both sides that the Salvadoran government could not protect the major cities and decisively defeat the FMLN and the FMLN could not gain control of the cities and provoke a massive uprising against the government. As a result, the two sides grew more receptive to mediation.

The results of a mutually hurting stalemate are that the parties will seek to deviate from their policies of fighting or coercion toward peaceful settlement. This is based on a cost-benefit calculation, consistent with a rational choice process of decision-making. In game theoretic terms, MHS is said to mark the transition point from a game of Prisoner's Dilemma to one of Chicken (Zartman, 2007a). Such a calculation makes sense if the supposed catastrophe is prospective and the players can see down the game tree and therefore negotiate in order to avoid an undesirable outcome.

With respect to the cost or "hurting" element, escalation to war is not necessarily a good indicator of the propensity for actors to seek out mediation. Greig (2005) notes that previous warfare alone between rival states is not significantly related to the likelihood of mediation taking place. Nevertheless, the broader history of relations between enduring rivals does appear to impact the likelihood of mediation; disputants, for example, are significantly more likely to request mediation as the duration of the rivalry increases and as the average severity level of the rivalry increases. Similarly, Ghosn (2010) notes that it is the combination of past rivalry and conflict intensity that provides the right mix to bring parties to a negotiating forum.

The above suggests that there are some cost elements from past interactions that promote mediation initiation, consistent with MHS logic. Nevertheless, there might be stronger evidence that current and prospective costs are far more influential to promoting mediation. Greig (2005) finds that mediation is far more likely during an ongoing militarized confrontation than as a result of prior conflict interactions; an enduring rivalry is more than five and a half times more likely to experience mediation during a month in which a militarized dispute is ongoing than it is when a dispute is absent. That is, actors are more sensitive to current costs than previous casualties or financial resources devoted to their confrontations with an enemy. Perhaps more importantly, the existence of ongoing violence and the risk of escalation might constitute a "precipice" in which actors fear future costs. Zartman (2000) points to the perception of a "precipice" among the disputants in which conditions are likely to deteriorate as a key force behind mediation. In this sense, mediation appears to operate as a form of triage in which the aim is simply to reduce the conflict that is currently underway before conditions further deteriorate; not only is mediation more likely to take place during an ongoing dispute, but it is also more likely to be requested by both disputants and more likely to be offered by a third party. Thus, disputants move toward mediation when they expect a better outcome with than without it and fear the consequences of continued confrontation (Princen, 1992; Pruitt, 2002; Regan, 2002). High-intensity conflict also helps soften the domestic audience costs that leaders face when entering into negotiations with an enemy. The pain of the conflict makes a leader's constituencies more tolerant of a negotiated settlement than if the costs of the conflict are abated (Beardsley, 2010).

Consistent with the idea of current threats and future costs is the finding that rival states that are contiguous are significantly more likely to attract mediation than non-contiguous rivals (Wilkenfeld et al., 2003; Greig, 2005; Beardsley, 2010). Disputes between contiguous states are more likely to escalate to war. As a result, because of the danger of intense conflict inherent to contiguous rivals and the greater divisibility of the issues under dispute between them, mediators may tend to be more drawn to the mediation of contiguous rivalries and contiguous rivals may feel a greater need for third-party intervention.

Considering the stalemate element, there are empirical findings that actors are less concerned with individual events and more so with future prospects. Greig (2005) finds that enduring state rivals are significantly less likely to request mediation as the level of stalemated outcomes in militarized confrontations mount; rivalries in which all previous disputes ended in stalemate (that is, neither side achieved its goals) are 54% less likely to request mediation than a rivalry in which no disputes have been stalemated. This suggests that high levels of stalemates function to embitter disputants more than encouraging them to move toward more conciliatory actions like mediation. Yet the *prospect* of stalemated outcomes in the future might drive parties to seek mediation. This might be indirectly indicated by the relative capabilities of the two enemies. When one actor is significantly more powerful than its opponent, it might anticipate victory in the long run and therefore no need to resort to mediation efforts, which could force it to compromise and accept a less favorable outcome. In contrast, two more evenly matched enemies might see the likelihood of prevailing as low and therefore pursue mediation to resolve their differences; a rivalry with power parity is nearly 65% more likely to request mediation than a rivalry in which there is a 5:1 power ratio between stronger and weaker parties (Greig, 2005).

Promise

The presence of significant costs alone may not be enough for rivals to seek diplomatic alternatives to their confrontations. They must also perceive that "a way out" of the rivalry exists – that is, that diplomatic opportunities and prospects exist (Zartman, 2000). This is largely a perceptual change in that little prevented the parties from pursuing mediation at prior junctures, and indeed third parties were almost assuredly available had the enemies signaled their willingness to come to the table. There are several sources for this perceptual change.

One way that enemies become more acceptant of diplomacy is from their past experience with it. When they meet at the bargaining table, through either mediation or direct negotiation, they have accepted in principle that diplomacy is a legitimate alternative. If such diplomatic efforts produce partial agreements which do not end the rivalry, they nevertheless lay the groundwork for future diplomatic efforts. In this way, diplomatic failure paradoxically may produce a greater likelihood of more meditation in the future. Thus, past diplomatic efforts will soften rivals to future negotiations, with the effect magnified if those past efforts produced partial settlements; nevertheless, the frequency of past mediations and therefore the acculturation to diplomatic management might be more important than the success of those previous efforts (Greig, 2005). Experience with the same mediator might also heighten this effect (Melin, 2011).

The stronger perception that mediation offers a way out might also come from forms of interaction between the rivals, other than past diplomatic efforts. Proponents of contact theory (Allport, 1954; Cook, 1971; Gartner et al., 1996; Amir, 1998; Pettigrew, 1998; Maoz, 2005) emphasize the influence that positive interactions between two adversaries play in softening the perceptions each has of the other and increasing the prospects for an improvement in their relations. In effect, positive interactions such as cooperation between the two sides can function to soften and change the adversarial views each holds of the other (Allport, 1954; Cook, 1984). By extension, this logic suggests that positive contacts between two sides might also increase their willingness to accept mediation and initiate a dialogue with one another. One way to achieve this might be greater cooperation between the rivals on issues outside of those under contention. Goertz and Diehl (2002) posit that international treaties in "functional" areas, beyond those underlying the rivalry, could promote better relations between states and perhaps lead to conflict management. That is, cooperation in certain areas softens up the rivals to diplomatic initiatives.

The diplomacy that followed the 1999 earthquakes in Greece and Turkey is a good example of how the cooperation described by contact theory can facilitate the opening of dialogue between parties in conflict (see more generally Akcinaroglu et al., 2011). Turkey and Greece have had a long-running, intense rivalry over disputed territory in the Mediterranean and over the status of Cyprus that, at various points in time, has been punctuated by crises and war. Turkey was struck by a large earthquake centered near the city of Izmit in August 1999. The earthquake killed thousands of Turks and left tens of thousands homeless. In response, the Greek government as well as groups within Greek civil society immediately supplied large amounts of relief assistance to Turkey, committing both resources and manpower to dealing with the disaster. In September 1999, a major earthquake hit Greece near Athens. The Turkish government, as their Greek counterparts had done one month earlier, gave extensive amounts of aid to help Greece deal with the disaster. Following this joint cooperation between Greece and Turkey, relations between the two sides warmed significantly, with them beginning a new round of negotiations over disputed issues, reaching agreement on Turkey's entrance to the EU, and even conducting joint military exercises in 2000 (Ker-Lindsay, 2000).

More than likely, it will take something more than incremental changes before long-time rivals begin to see mediation as a preferable alternative to fighting. It might be that perceptions only change after a dramatic event, such as the presence of an "external shock," which creates the opportunity for parties to revise entrenched perceptions about opponents (Mooradian and Druckman, 1999). Without significant changes in either the political or strategic make-up of rivals, rivalries stabilize around a general pattern of conflictual interaction. This stasis can be broken by the occurrence of political shifts within the rivals that create an opening for the reevaluation of the policies of enduring rivals. Stein and Lewis (1996), for example, argue that regime changes can assist in reviving stalled negotiations and launching new peace initiatives. These can include changes in the type of regime, new methods of leadership selection, or changes in the size of the leadership selectorate. As these political changes occur, a wide range of policy beliefs and assumptions tend to be reevaluated and replaced. Yet this might not produce an immediate effect (for example, within a month – see Ghosn, 2010) as the process of policy reevaluation and change is likely to take some time; leaders usually have other immediate priorities relative to opening negotiations with an enemy and thus accepting mediation is unlikely to be one their first acts when assuming power. In general, any change in regimes might prompt more mediation, but those that result in democratic regimes have the greatest effect for the reasons noted below.

Other Willingness Factors
Beyond the impact of conflict pain and promise, some other factors make actors inclined to accept mediation. Although the grievance and animosity built up between two sides can make getting them to the bargaining table difficult, the political characteristics of the contending sides shape in important ways their amenability to accepting mediation. There is substantial evidence in the scholarly literature that democratic disputants are more likely to accept offers of mediation than

non-democracies (Bercovitch et al., 1991; Dixon, 1994; Greig, 2005; Raymond, 1994). Among democracies, the same norms that encourage negotiation and compromise over contentious domestic political issues also encourage the use of diplomacy to handle international disputes.

Although all rivalries are theoretically susceptible to mediation, in practice some types of rivalries are unlikely to experience mediation. In particular, rivalries in which there is at least one major power are unlikely to attract mediation. Major power states such as the United States or the Soviet Union/Russia, however, face a different decision calculus in agreeing to mediation. Few principal mediators are likely to have the leverage or the ability to offer the resources necessary to change the bargaining dynamic between the disputants in ways sufficient to foster agreement when it would not otherwise take place.

Getting to Agreement

Although the assistance of a willing mediator and the consent of the conflicting sides to sit down and talk is an important initial step toward peace, it is by no means a guarantee that a settlement can be reached and peace established. Indeed, most mediation efforts are unsuccessful. In our sample, more than 55% of all mediation efforts failed. This failure rate, however, has varied considerably over time. Mediation efforts during the Cold War, although less frequently applied, tended to have a much higher success rate than mediation efforts after the Cold War. For both civil and interstate conflicts, the mediation failure rate was highest during the 1950s and 1980s. Clearly, simply getting parties in conflict together at the bargaining table is often not enough to produce peace.

In an ideal world, participating in a peace process would be a clear indicator that the two sides in a conflict are ready to take steps necessary to achieve an agreement that ends their fighting. Yet, disputants often engage in mediation for reasons beyond managing their conflict. Belligerents may accept mediation, even if they have little interest in a settlement, in order to appease a powerful third party that is offering diplomatic intervention. In such cases, unless the third party can provide sufficient incentives to the two sides once they get to the bargaining table to make them more amenable to a settlement, the mediation effort will fail. Conflicting sides can also see more opportunistic benefits from mediation. At the height of a conflict, accepting mediation can improve a belligerent's public reputation while also buying them time and breathing space in which to mobilize their forces and improve their prospects on the battlefield (Richmond, 1998). Mediation efforts in which the contending sides enter the talks with these "devious objectives" are likely to be doomed to failure, regardless of the mediating capabilities of the third party. Instead, the best recipe for successful mediation, while still no guarantee of success, includes both a skilled and effective mediator and warring sides that are genuinely motivated to settle their conflict.

The factors that impact the success or failure of mediation are varied. One way to examine them is through the framework of the "contingency model of mediation" (Bercovitch and Jackson, 2009). There, mediation outcomes are a function of both contextual factors (characteristics of the mediator, disputants, conflict) and the process (e.g. timing and other concerns) of the mediation. It is often the complex interaction of these factors that determines whether a mediation effort will be successful and to what degree.

Mediator Attributes

The third party providing mediation plays an important role in the success and failure of mediation, but there is no one size fits all for every conflict. The communication facilitation approach adopted by the Norwegian mediation team during the Oslo peace process, by opening closed communication linkages, fit the needs of the Israelis and the Palestinians at the time. Because of the important religious role played by the Pope in Chile and Argentina, Vatican mediation during the Beagle Channel Dispute was effective in preventing a war and establishing a settlement after a long period of talks. Swapping mediators between these two conflicts would likely produce very different outcomes to the talks. Yet, despite the uniqueness of individual conflicts, the mediation literature has gained insight into some general patterns that link the characteristics of the third party providing mediation to the outcome of the talks. These most notably reflect the characteristics of the mediating actor, but there is an indication that the strategies adopted by the mediator have some impact as well.

Powerful mediators can bring resources to bear upon a mediation process that can produce success where a less powerful mediator might fail. Major power mediators, for example, can serve as "mediators with muscle," using their power as leverage to encourage and cajole disputants toward agreement (Touval, 1992; Crocker et al., 1999). In doing so, powerful mediators can apply their resources to raise the costs for disputants rejecting a settlement, increase their benefits of signing an agreement, and provide mechanisms to ensure compliance with any agreement reached. Major power states can also use their intelligence gathering capabilities as a means to improve their mediation efforts, increasing their ability to communicate information about the conflict to the disputants (Rauchhaus, 2006). The Camp David talks between Israel and Egypt benefited not only from the dissatisfaction with the status quo of Israel and Egypt, but also from the ability of the United States to use its power over both countries to leverage an agreement (Stein and Lewis, 1996).

Not only does the identity of the actor that a particular mediator represents shape the outcome of mediation, but the status of the individual conducting the mediation also influences the prospects for success. High-ranking mediators can improve the chances for mediation success because they bring greater prestige and leverage to the mediation than lower-ranking mediators (Low, 1985; Zartman and Touval, 1985; Bercovitch and Houston, 1993). A mediation effort led by an American president conveys much greater gravitas, prestige, and power than one led by an American ambassador, even though both efforts are backed by the power of the American government. High-ranking mediators can use their status as a form of social influence that provides an additional source of leverage that can be vital in extracting concessions from parties in conflict (Bercovitch and Houston, 1993; Bercovitch, 1997).

The previous discussion might imply that states, and in particular powerful ones, are the most successful mediators. In fact, mediation by international organizations (IGOs) is more often successful than that conducted by a state (more than 50% more successful) or coalitions of states (Frazier and Dixon, 2009). This is attributed to the greater legitimacy and trust ascribed to IGOs by conflict parties; in contrast, state mediators might be suspected of ulterior motives and of protecting their own interests when assuming the alleged third-party role.

The conventional characterization of the mediator is as an unbiased arbiter between the two sides, acceptable to both sides because she is seen as fair. A substantial body of research has challenged both the necessity and desirability of an unbiased mediator. Rauchhaus (2006) finds that both biased and unbiased mediators can be effective, although impartial mediators are more likely to be successful. Others (Touval, 1975; Smith, 1985; Touval and Zartman, 1985a; Jabri, 1990) argue that an impartial mediator is not a prerequisite for successful mediation. According to their logic, even mediators with clear interests at stake in a conflict can play an effective role in proposing solutions and communicating information to the disputants.

Some scholars (Kydd, 2003; 2006; Favretto, 2009) argue that mediator bias can even be beneficial for an agreement. Because they have a stake in the conflict, biased third parties are more likely to produce successful mediation results. According to this logic, although disputants may question the fairness of a biased mediator, the interests that a biased mediator has in a conflict encourage the third party to maximize the effort and resources it commits to mediating the dispute and see the peace agreement through implementation. This bias and commitment to implementation is what makes the United States an especially valuable mediator of the Israeli–Palestinian conflict. Because of long-run American interests in the region and the parties, both sides can anticipate continued American involvement in the implementation of any agreement reached. Along these same lines, mediator bias could increase the likelihood of peaceful settlement because the interests that produce the bias serve to convince the disputants that the third party will remain engaged after a settlement is reached and enforce the agreement by military means, if necessary. The suitability of a biased or unbiased mediator will thus vary by context, and it is difficult to draw generalizations that apply to all or most situations.

Mediators employ different strategies reflective of their perception of what the conflict requires as well as the resources and expertise that the mediator brings to the table. These range from relatively low intervention strategies (consisting of more limited mediator involvement) to high-intervention strategies, in which the mediator engages in a range of activities. Bercovitch et al. (1991) classify three types of strategies on this kind of scale. Communication-facilitation strategies envision a more passive role for the mediation, largely keeping channels of information open and passing along information to the disputants. This strategy generally has the lowest success rate (Bercovitch and Regan, 2004). Nevertheless, even within this category, there is variation. Those actors with high information capacity (generally larger states with ties to the disputants) are more effective than those with low capacity (Savun, 2009). Procedural strategies involve a larger role for the mediator, often controlling the process of mediation, such as the agenda, location for the mediation, and the timing and frequency of negotiation sessions. These strategies tend to be more effective than less intrusive, communication-centered roles. The highest level of involvement occurs with directive strategies. This involves suggesting terms of settlement and offering incentives, among other strategies, in order to achieve an agreement. Even though directive strategies still fail over half of the time, they are notably the most successful in achieving partial and full settlements (Bercovitch and Regan, 2004).

Mediation efforts fail for many reasons. Some fail because the third party is ineffective and lacks sufficient trust among the two sides to facilitate a settlement. In general, mediators are likely to be most effective when they bring something to the mediation process that alters the dynamics between the conflicting parties. For some mediators, this can be resources that serve to sweeten a potential deal between the two sides or provide a means of ensuring compliance with an agreement that is reached. For other mediators, it is their ability to improve the communication lines between the conflicting sides and allow them to locate potential areas of agreement that might otherwise go unrecognized by the two sides that plays a decisive role in fostering a successful mediation outcome. A mediator that lacks the ability, either because of her own lack of mediation skills and experience or because

of lack of trust by the belligerents, to improve communications between the two sides is unlikely to produce a successful
outcome. Even the most effective mediator will be unable to
achieve mediation success when finding herself mediating a
conflict in which the two sides are unwilling to make the concessions necessary for a mediated settlement or take the steps
necessary to diminish their conflict. Accordingly, there are a
variety of other factors that influence mediation success and
failure.

Timing Issues
Assuming that a capable, willing mediator is available to
manage a conflict and the parties are open to accepting
mediation, when do warring sides become most amenable
to making concessions and achieving a diplomatic settlement to their conflict? There has been considerable debate on
when during the life cycle of a conflict is the most desirable
point for diplomatic intervention; much of this focuses on
whether mediation should occur "early" or "late" in the conflict. Empirically, advocates of both positions might be correct.
There is considerable evidence (Greig, 2001; Regan and Stam,
2000) of a curvilinear relationship between mediation timing
and its ultimate impact on the conflict; mediations attempted
early or late tend to reduce the duration of conflict. In contrast,
mediations attempted after the initial opening, but before the
latter stages of a dispute actually contribute to lengthening
the conflict, rather than resolving it. Thus, mediation can be
successful before the disputants have built up high levels of
hostility that make compromises difficult. Furthermore, such
early success can have longer-term consequences as conflict can be moderated even in long-standing state rivalries
(Andersen et al., 2001). To understand the timing of when
belligerents will be most motivated toward a mediated settlement, it is important to understand the link between conflict

and diplomacy. War is a strategic policy tool by which an actor seeks to impose costs upon an opposing side that are sufficient to make it acquiesce to the actor's demands or unable to resist the actor's ability to impose them unilaterally. This Clausewitzian view of war is bedrock to rational choice perspectives on the occurrence of inter- and intrastate conflict and the conditions under which these conflicts are settled. In effect, during conflict the use of violence between two sides is a form of bargaining in which each attempts to outbid the other through violence, and seeks to convince the other that the costs of resistance are higher than yielding and agreeing to the terms being demanded. War ends when the two sides each recognize that the agreement that they can produce at the bargaining table is preferable to their expected outcome from continued fighting (Fearon, 1995; Wagner, 2000; Slantchev, 2004).

We noted above that mutually hurting stalemates provide the impetus or "push" for negotiations to begin, but there need to be some additional factors beyond cost considerations in order to encourage the parties to settle. Violence tends to foster further violence as warring sides see their prior conflict costs as sunk costs, further encouraging them to commit future resources to win the conflict and achieve a return on those sunk costs (Mitchell, 2000). This momentum toward more violence is further exacerbated by the tendency of actors to grow more risk-acceptant when facing potential losses over issues salient to them – precisely the type of issues over which war is most likely in the first place – an effect noted by prospect theory (see, for example, Levy, 1997; Davis, 2000; Jervis, 2004). At the same time, prior violence also brings with it consequences for the belligerents that further sustain armed conflict. Although two sides may initially see the use of violence as a strategic choice by which to best achieve their goals, war often develops a momentum of its own as the aims of the belligerents shift from simply achieving their policy goals toward also punishing the adversary (Zartman, 2000). Belligerents involved in long-running, high-intensity conflicts are especially likely to experience this effect. As the two sides continue to fight one another, their grievances deepen and their level of animosity toward one another grows, heightening the degree to which both sides see one another as not only opponents, but as evil (Aggestam and Jonsson, 1997). At the same time, in order to continue to extract from their people the resources necessary to win the conflict, leaders reinforce this enemy image within their populace, recognizing that framing a conflict in "us vs. them" terms is an important means of mobilizing and maintaining support for the war effort (Spector, 1998). Put together, these forces tend to push parties in conflict toward seeing their conflict as one of good versus evil, a position that makes negotiating with the other side difficult and settlement of the conflict virtually impossible.

Even when a mutually hurting stalemate exists between the two sides, it may be difficult for the belligerents to recognize its presence and even more problematic for them to act upon it. In an unwinnable conflict, both sides may believe that if they can only redouble their efforts and devote more resources to the fight, victory can still be found. It might take an exceptionally serious conflict or repeated failures to resolve the conflict by force before the warring parties are willing to settle. Mooradian and Druckman (1999) note that mediation efforts between Armenia and Azerbaijan over Nagorno-Karabakh were largely ineffective until 1994. Before the conflict escalated to the level of a hurting stalemate, both sides believed that they retained the ability to impose a settlement over the Nagorno-Karabakh issue through military victory. Only when they suffered considerable military losses as a result of severe conflict in late 1993 and early 1994 was the tide turned and the foundation set for successful conflict management between Armenia and Azerbaijan. Crocker (1992) observes a similar effect in the relations between Angola and South Africa. A series of recurring mediations occurred between the rivals between 1981 and 1987. Yet, movement on the issues under dispute and reduction in the level of conflict did not occur until 1987. Crocker argues that it was the escalation of military conflict in 1987 that fostered successful mediation and ultimately resulted in the withdrawal of Cuban troops from Angola and South African troops from Namibia.

Even when the contending sides grow weary of fighting and see their conflict as unwinnable, the domestic risks and political costs of negotiating with the adversary may be seen as simply too high for either side to make a peace overture toward the other side. For these reasons, Zartman (1989; 2000) emphasizes the important role of "ripeness" as a key set of conditions under which settlement becomes possible among two conflicting sides. In this respect, ripeness is best thought of as a concatenation of conditions under which the prospects for successful negotiation and settlement of the conflict grow more favorable. The pain and stalemate of an intractable conflict are not enough to induce the parties toward a settlement. Instead, the two sides must also either see themselves at a juncture in which they have narrowly missed a disaster produced by the conflict or recognize the danger of one occurring in the future if the conflict continues unabated. The 2001–2002 crisis between India and Pakistan that was precipitated by the December 13 militant attack on the Indian Parliament is a good example. Following that attack, India mobilized troops to Kashmir and Punjab, the largest such mobilization since their 1971 war. Pakistan responded in kind, deploying approximately 120,000 troops near the Line of Control in Kashmir. This crisis pattern was similar to previous flare-ups in tensions between the two long-running rivals, tensions that had produced war on several occasions. Conditions further deteriorated between the two sides following an armed attack by gunmen on an Indian army camp near Jammu and several deadly skirmishes between Indian and Pakistani troops along the Kashmir frontier in May 2002. Unlike in previous crises between India and Pakistan, both countries had nuclear weapons in 2002, raising the stakes dramatically if full-scale war were to break out. Thus, the nuclear capabilities of the two sides, by threatening devastation to the two countries and their population centers, provided the precipice that was vital in encouraging the two sides to demobilize their troops and reach a cease-fire.

Zartman (1989; 2000; 2007b) also points to the important role that the perception of a "mutually enticing opportunity (MEO)" by the two parties plays in the emergence of ripeness. Contending sides may strongly desire a means to transition their relationship away from continued violence toward peace, but progress will be impossible if they have little hope that such a change is possible. For the two sides, leaders with sufficient power are vital to the development of a belief that a way out is possible in the conflict. Improvement in relations between Israel and Egypt following the series of Arab–Israeli wars was only possible because Egyptian President Anwar Sadat, recognizing that the Egyptian economy could no longer bear the strain from continued war with Israel, had sufficient political power at home to declare his willingness to "go anywhere" for peace with Israel. Similarly, progress was only possible because Israel's Begin-led government had enough political strength to respond favorably to Sadat's overture, yielding a process that saw Sadat address the Israeli Knesset and culminating with the Camp David Accords and the establishment of peace between Israel and Egypt.

If belligerents were always able to create, recognize, and act upon ripe conditions for settling their conflict, third-party conflict management would never be necessary. Instead of mediating their conflict, bilateral negotiations would be sufficient to establish peace and produce a settlement. Yet, especially in the longest-running, most deadly conflicts, the assistance of a mediator is necessary to create a way out for the belligerents. A mediator can help reestablish communications between the two sides, linkages that are often frayed, if not destroyed entirely, as a conflict continues. In doing so, the mediator can communicate the goals and expectations of the two sides, helping them to recognize areas of potential agreement and see possibilities for settlement that may not be obvious to them through bilateral talks. Because a third party can bring resources to the talks that can be important in making an agreement more palatable to the two sides, a mediator can also enhance the parties' perceptions of diplomatic alternatives by making previously rejected settlement terms more acceptable.

Not only can third parties act upon ripe conditions, they can also induce ripeness in a conflict, making conditions that were previously not conducive to settlement more favorable. One way in which a third party can induce ripeness in an otherwise unripe conflict is to make the pain felt by the belligerents more acute and both sides' inability to win the conflict more apparent. The decision by Henry Kissinger to slow the supply of resources to Israel during the Yom Kippur War was an effort to heighten the Israeli sense of a looming costly stalemate, making them more amenable to a mediated settlement to the conflict (Richter, 1992). Ironically, sometimes third-party steps that contribute to more violence in the short run are needed to encourage the ripeness necessary to effect a long-term mediated settlement. The American decision to support arming Bosnian Muslims and Croats during the Bosnian War is a good example of this at work (Rieff, 1995). Although arming the Bosnian Muslims and Croats no doubt increased the intensity of the fighting and the death and destruction produced by the war, it was done with an eye toward increasing the conflict costs felt by the Bosnian Serbs and reducing their beliefs that they could win the war and impose their own settlement terms.

A more extreme third-party effort to induce ripeness in a conflict was the NATO bombing effort against Serbia during the Kosovo War. Rather than simply providing support to one side in the conflict as a means of producing a balance between the two sides and establishing a hurting stalemate that makes both sides more amenable to talks, the NATO bombing campaign sought to impose conflict costs directly on the Serbian side (Allen and Vincent, 2011). By bombing Serbian cities, military installations, and troop positions, NATO raised the costs of continued Serbian unwillingness to withdraw its forces from Kosovo and agree to the terms spelled out at Rambaouillet. In this respect, seventy-eight days of NATO bombing served to alter the strategic calculations of the Serbs, making acceptable settlement terms that were previously rejected by the Serbs.

Although the concept of ripeness offers considerable intuitive appeal for understanding when conflicts are most amenable for settlement, it has received some criticism. One objection rests on the risk of a circular argument in linking ripeness to mediation success (Kleiboer, 1994). If mediation is successful because conditions are ripe and, in turn, successful mediation is an indicator of the presence of ripeness, then ripeness is tautological, providing no additional information beyond mediation success. Treatments of ripeness such as that described by Zartman (1989; 2000) avoid tautology by arguing that ripeness is neither necessary nor sufficient for mediation success. Instead, ripeness increases the chances that a mediated agreement can be reached. Ripe moments can pass without agreement if there is not a capable mediator available to help manage the conflict or if the mediation effort is ineffectively done. At the same time, a skilled mediator can foster agreement even when ripeness is not present, by increasing the sense among the conflicting sides that conditions are likely to grow worse and the conflict is unsustainable.

A second criticism of ripeness concerns its focus on necessary conditions and the joint thinking of the two sides in conflict (Pruitt, 2007). Instead, "readiness theory" (Pruitt, 2005; 2007) expands upon ripeness by arguing that one must look at the motivation disputants have to settle their conflict and the level of optimism they have for the outcome of diplomacy. Unlike ripeness, which sees the development of a mutually hurting stalemate and the sense of a "way out" as necessary conditions that are prerequisites for settlement, the components of readiness theory are multiplicative and can partially substitute for one another. As a result, a high level of motivation to settle can make up for a lower level of diplomatic optimism and vice versa.

Readiness theory shows some similarity to the elements of ripeness described by Zartman (1989; 2000). The MEO perceived by conflicting parties that Zartman sees as important for the development of ripeness is similar to Pruitt's (2005) view of optimism for diplomacy in readiness theory. There are, however, key differences between these two forces of diplomatic optimism. For Zartman, both sides must perceive the presence of a diplomatic way out for ripeness to develop. For Pruitt, readiness can occur when only one side becomes optimistic about the effects of diplomacy because, once that sense of optimism develops, that side becomes more motivated to make significant concessions to the less optimistic side. This optimism can develop when the contending sides become less ambitious in their goals for the conflict, develop greater levels of trust with one another, or increasingly conclude that the framework for a potential agreement is emergent (Pruitt, 2007).

Conflict Context

Implicit within both ripeness and readiness theory is that the conflict context conditions the success and failure of mediation. As events on the battlefield unfold, the conflicting parties gauge the success and failure of violence as a means to achieve their goals and weigh the benefits of shifting their strategies toward diplomatic solutions. There is not necessarily a substantial difference between mediation success rates in interstate versus civil conflicts. About 35% of all civil war mediations result in partial or full agreement, while nearly 34% of all interstate conflict mediations achieve a similar level of success. More telling is the severity of the conflict and issues over which it is fought.

Consistent with Zartman's (2000) argument that the development of a hurting stalemate facilitates mediation success, a considerable number of studies (Jackson, 1952; Young, 1967; Regan and Stam, 2000; Greig, 2001) have found that conflict severity affects the willingness of disputants to accept mediation and reach a settlement. Conflicts with the fewest fatalities show a higher propensity to achieve a full settlement than those with higher levels of deaths. In conflicts with between 0 and 1,000 fatalities, approximately 15% of all mediation efforts result in full settlement. In contrast, that rate drops by half for conflicts with a fatality level between 5,001 and 10,000 deaths. The chances for future settlement are even smaller in conflicts at the highest level of severity; in conflicts producing more than 10,000 deaths, less than 4% of all mediation efforts result in a full settlement. Paradoxically, intense conflict might bring parties to the table, but it might also undermine the possibility of a comprehensive agreement. Yet the primary differences in mediation outcomes for different levels of conflict severity only exist for full settlements. That is, the conflict context in terms of casualties does not affect the propensity for achieving simple cease-fires or partial settlements.

Beyond the severity of a conflict, mediation success is also heavily dependent on the issues in dispute between the enemies. Certain kinds of disputes are more difficult to handle than others. Not surprisingly, multidimensional disputes with complex issues are often harder to resolve than those with a single issue or when the conflict is more narrowly confined (Bercovitch and Langley, 1993). Conflict issues most prone to escalation are those involving competing territorial claims (Senese and Vasquez, 2008), but counter-intuitively certain territorial concerns might be more amenable to mediation (Greig, 2001). Territory is inherently divisible and therefore subject to compromise, aiding the possibility of a mediated settlement. Yet some disputed territories (e.g. Jerusalem, Kashmir) have intangible value for the disputants, primarily for their religious or historical associations (Hensel and Mitchell, 2005). These are more difficult to resolve in that the "win set" of acceptable outcomes for both parties might be empty; that is, there might be no solution, mediated or otherwise, that both sides will accept.

Conflict Parties
As important as the mediator, the timing of the mediation, and the conflict context might be, it is tempting to forget that it is the disputing parties that are the ones who must agree to any settlement. Indeed, mediation is more successful when one or more of the parties initiates the diplomatic process (Greig, 2001; Bercovitch and DeRouen, 2005). Accordingly, there are certain aspects of those enemies and associated actors that help determine mediation success or failure.

One key factor, central to most models of international behavior, is the power distribution between the disputing parties. The development of a mutually hurting stalemate requires not only high costs, but also an inability of each of the two sides to overcome the other on the battlefield and impose their preferred solution to the conflict. Consistent with this logic, a sizeable stream of research has found that power parity between conflicting parties increases the prospects for successful mediation (Zartman, 1981; Touval, 1982; Bercovitch, 1989; Kriesberg, 1992). Under power parity, two sides throw their resources at one another on the battlefield, only to recognize gradually that they are evenly matched and unable to impose their will on the other side. Just less than 9% of all mediation efforts among actors with equal levels of power result in a full settlement, while only 6% of all mediation attempts among unequal actors achieve the same level of success. Conflicts among equals are also more likely to achieve partial agreements and cease-fires than conflicts with an unequal distribution of power. At power parity, 47% of all mediation efforts are unsuccessful. By contrast, 57% of all mediation attempts among unequal actors are unsuccessful.

The effect of power parity on mediation success appears to have a notable exception and also depends upon the type of conflict involved. Major power states, who are generally comparable in military and other capabilities, are not only less likely to avail themselves of mediation as noted earlier in the chapter, but also are less successful in achieving settlements when mediation does occur (Frazier and Dixon, 2009). Furthermore, among interstate conflicts, power parity has little effect upon the likelihood of achieving a full settlement. In civil conflicts, power parity both increases the likelihood of full settlement and reduces the likelihood of failure overall.

In addition to their attributes, the prior relationships of the disputants influence the prospects for mediation success and these can be positive or negative. Just as disputants learn from what happens on the battlefield and use that information to decide whether to accept mediation and reach a settlement, they also learn from what happens at the bargaining table. As indicated above, the more often mediation is used in the past, the more likely it is to be accepted in the future by rival states (Greig and Diehl, 2006). Similarly, Regan and Stam (2000) note a cumulative effect of mediation on the relations between states in conflict such that the more often mediation occurs, the more likely it becomes to reduce the duration of interstate disputes. Recurring mediation efforts can also lay the groundwork for future mediation success by providing disputants with an opportunity to develop a rapport with one another and the mediator (Zubek et al., 1992).

Past mediation experiences with one another can lay the groundwork for a mediated settlement, but this can be counteracted by prior negative experiences. Most notably with respect to states and other actors, being involved in an enduring rivalry can enhance the likelihood that mediation will occur, but the latter is notably less successful in those contexts (Bercovitch and Diehl, 1997). Still, success is possible in this context, with short-term agreements most likely early in the rivalry and the prospects for long-term changes better in the latter stages of rivalry (Greig, 2001). Nevertheless, the buildup of hostility and past negative interactions make this a difficult context in which to achieve diplomatic progress.

Mediated negotiations are sometimes influenced by actors other than the primary parties to the disputes. Actors external to the conflict can put pressure on the disputants to settle (or not), and the impact of such efforts will be mitigated or enhanced by the ties between all the parties and the leverage exercised by those outside actors (Touval, 2000). Most attention, however, has been devoted to "spoilers." Spoilers are actors that seek to derail a peace process because they see the peace being developed as less favorable to their interests than the conflictual status quo. During the Lebanese Civil

War, groups that profited from smuggling, drug trafficking, and extortion rackets in the chaos caused by the violence had few incentives to participate in a settlement and many more reasons to prevent the achievement of peace (Wennmann, 2009). Spoilers vary in the level of incompatibility between their interests and the effects of a peace agreement. This level of incompatibility can range from that of a limited spoiler that seeks narrow goals in effecting change in the terms of a peace agreement to a total spoiler, who holds unchangeable goals that are wholly incompatible with the terms of the peace agreement (Stedman, 1997). Because of its unyielding unwillingness to accept any Israeli–Palestinian settlement terms that recognize Israel's right to exist, Hamas is a good example of a total spoiler.

Spoilers can impact a peace process in two ways. First, violence by spoilers seeks to prevent moderates from reaching a settlement. Spoilers seek to derail settlements by encouraging mistrust between moderates on both sides of a conflict, exacerbating the doubts that each side has about the other's willingness to negotiate in good faith (Kydd and Walter, 2002). As spoilers launch their attacks, it becomes increasingly difficult for moderates on their side to convince opposition moderates that they are sincere in the pursuit of peace. As these doubts deepen, it grows harder for any settlement to be reached between the two sides. For example, bombings by Irish Republican Army (IRA) splinter groups during the Northern Ireland peace process made it difficult for IRA representatives to convince the unionist side that they sincerely sought peace and were not simply feigning peaceful intentions while continuing to employ violence.

Second, even if spoilers cannot prevent an agreement from being reached, they can undermine its implementation. Just as spoiler violence can raise mistrust about whether moderates are bargaining in good faith, this same mistrust can also cause disputants to question whether the other side will live up to the terms of an agreement (Kydd and Walter, 2002). Because parties in conflict fear exploitation, spoiler violence can be seen as a signal of cheating on an agreement by the other side, causing the collapse of an agreement that is otherwise supported by moderates on both sides. In general, however, spoilers are better able to derail peace talks from reaching an agreement than to undermine an agreement once it has been reached. In her study of civil conflicts, Nilsson (2008) finds that spoilers are effective in disrupting peace processes, but do not impact the commitment of signatories of a peace agreement to follow through with implementation. In this respect, it seems that once parties commit to an agreement, the ability of spoilers to sow sufficient mistrust among them to prevent implementation of the agreement is limited.

There are a number of ways of dealing with spoilers to a peace process. Carrots and sticks can be offered to spoilers, providing them with incentives to sign on to a settlement and punishments for the continued usage of violence (Stedman, 1997). Citizen support for a peace process, by backing the peace efforts of moderates, can also play an important role in short-circuiting the effectiveness of spoilers by either marginalizing them or persuading them to embrace peace (Kydd and Walter, 2002). Third parties can help undermine the effect of spoilers on a peace process. They can provide information to moderates on each side, reducing the uncertainty that spoiler violence causes and reassuring participants in the peace process of the sincerity of the other side (Kydd and Walter, 2002).

The risk of spoilers grows as the number of parties involved in a conflict increases. Conflicts involving a large number of parties are substantially less likely to reach a full settlement than conflicts involving just two parties. In conflicts with just two parties, 8% of all mediation efforts result in a full settlement. By contrast, in conflicts involving more than ten parties only 1% of mediation attempts achieve a full settlement. Nevertheless, conflicts involving the largest number of parties are actually the least likely to experience failed mediation. Instead, these conflicts are more likely to achieve a mediated cease-fire than any other conflict. This is consistent with the effect of spoilers on peace agreements. For conflicts involving the greatest number of actors, there may be sufficient will present to manage the conflict and establish a cease-fire, but the barriers to a full or partial settlement are too strong.

One barrier to successful mediation is getting the parties to the bargaining table under conditions when mediation is most likely to be successful. In general, however, third parties do not offer mediation when it is apt to be fruitful (Greig, 2005). This disconnect between the timing of mediation and its success is problematic for two reasons. First, it suggests that third parties waste time and energy offering mediation to disputants when it is unlikely to yield positive results. Failed mediation efforts, in turn, run the risk of convincing disputants of the impossibility of managing their conflict, potentially spoiling future mediation efforts. Second, because third parties do not offer mediation when it is most likely to be successful, those conflicts that need third-party assistance the most may not receive the assistance of a mediator when they most need it unless they ask for it. The distinction between the conditions under which mediation tends to be applied to conflicts and the conditions under which it is successful accounts for some of the reasons why, although mediation is such a commonly used conflict management tool, it fails so often.

The Development of an MHS during the Iran–Iraq War

On September 22, 1980 Iraq launched a full-scale invasion of Iran, attacking Iranian airfields and concentrating the largest thrust of its invasion force against Iranian territory along its southern border with Iraq near the strategically vital Shatt al-Arab Waterway. The roots of the conflict were linked to both short- and long-term disputes between the two countries, with competition and internal interference between the two sides dating back to the days of the Ottoman and Persian Empires (Hiro, 1991). In the short term, territorial disputes between Iran and Iraq over the borders of their Kurdish territories, control and navigation of the Shatt al-Arab Waterway, and competition for regional leadership were the core sources of dispute that provided the impetus for war (Johnson, 2011). The assassination attempt against Iraqi Deputy Prime Minister Tariq Aziz, a plot that was seen by Iraq as Iranian-inspired, provided the pretext for Iraq's invasion. More broadly speaking, the decision by Iraqi President Saddam Hussein to invade Iran in 1980 was motivated by fears of a Shia revolt in southern Iraq inspired by Iran's 1979 Shia revolution, an effort by Iraq to establish itself as the preeminent power in the region following Egypt's peace agreement with Israel, and the drive to settle the Shatt al-Arab issue once and for all on terms favorable for Iraq (Johnson, 2011).

Although the Iranian response to the invasion was initially chaotic, by the second day of the conflict Iran had established air superiority and begun to mount a better coordinated response to the Iraqi invasion (Karsh, 2002). By early 1981, the conflict had ground to a stalemate with neither side able to overwhelm the other. Iran would attempt to break the stalemate with successful offensives in 1982, but by 1983 the conflict had again fallen into a costly stalemate between the two sides. With neither side able to overcome the other on the battlefield, each turned to the use of chemical weapons against the other and began conducting strategic bombing and missile attacks against the other's population centers, further heightening the costs of the conflict.

Mediation during the Iran–Iraq War offers a good example of the way in which, once one of the belligerents sours upon mediation, conflict intensifies and conflict management grows more difficult. Several efforts to mediate the conflict in 1981 and 1982 were conducted by the United Nations, the Islamic Conference Organization (OIC), and states representing the non-aligned movement. Denied the quick victory that it had anticipated, Iraq accepted cease-fire proposals offered by the OIC in late 1980 and reiterated its willingness to agree to a cease-fire and negotiate in 1982 (Hume, 1994; Souresrafil, 1989). Because Iran saw the only just way to end the war as a total victory over Iraq that punished its aggression and removed its political leadership, these diplomatic efforts yielded little progress (Souresrafil, 1989). Indeed, by August 1981, Iran had grown so convinced that mediation was likely to be fruitless that Iranian president Mohammed Radjai informed the visiting mediation delegation from the Non-Aligned Movement that the delegation had "not been very useful in clarifying the stance of the aggressor and the situation of the nation against which the aggression has taken place" and emphasized that Iran would "decide the fate of the war on the battlefield" (*Keesings*, 1982: 31523).

A deeper blow to efforts to mediate the Iran–Iraq War occurred in 1982. After working with Iran and Iraq for over a year, Algerian mediators had arguably made more progress than any other third party in managing the conflict. On May 4, 1982, a plane traveling between Baghdad and Tehran carrying the Algerian Foreign Minister and his mediation team inexplicably crashed. Iran accused Iraq of shooting down the plane and immediately adopted a much tougher line against Iraq, demanding the removal of Saddam Hussein's regime and, in July 1982, expanding the war into Iraqi territory. Efforts to mediate the conflict by the Gulf Cooperation Council (GCC) through 1985 were similarly fruitless, with the inability of either side to alter the enemy images they held of the other, preventing any progress toward settlement (Ayres, 1997). The war did not end until six years later when both sides ultimately sought compromise largely because of war-weariness, but not before producing more than 700,000 battlefield deaths and refugees in the millions, as well as costing each side billions of dollars in treasure.

What is most striking about the experience of the Iran–Iraq War is that the solution to the conflict that was ultimately accepted in 1988 was nearly the same as that initially proposed by Ambassador Eliasson's UN team in 1980 (Eliasson, 2002). Because both sides eschewed diplomatic efforts in favor of continued conflict, however, each was forced to bear high conflict costs for eight years that might otherwise have been avoided. In this respect, once warring parties conclude that mediation is likely to be ineffective in producing an acceptable settlement, it becomes exceedingly difficult to encourage conflict management until the pain from the battlefield becomes unbearable.

Iranian acceptance of a cease-fire in mid 1988 was a sudden development that was rooted in its perception of the conflict as a hurting stalemate in which it expected its costs and pain to deepen and its prospects for success on the battlefield to deteriorate. As recently as September 1987, Iranian President Khamenei saw few benefits for Iran in agreeing to a ceasefire, stating in an address to the United Nations General Assembly:

> [T]he kind of peace approved by the Iraqi regime today would, after a few years or whenever it suspected to be in a strong position, evaporate in a moment, and another war would engulf the region. The only guarantee for the future is punishment of the aggressor.
>
> (Hume, 1994: 121).

Yet, from the latter part of 1987 onward, conditions worsened for Iran, making acceptance of UN Resolution 598, which called for a cease-fire between the two sides, more attractive for Iran. Despite announcing a major planned offensive in 1987, no offensive followed as Iran was unable to meet its manpower goals and the Iranian military suffered from significant equipment and munitions shortages (Johnson, 2011). As a result of losses on the battlefield, Iran lost a sizeable portion of its armor capability and, following clashes with the United States navy during the Tanker War in 1988, lost half of its navy (Hume, 1994). Not only had Iran suffered significant setbacks on the battlefield (withdrawing from all of the Iraqi territory it held in April 1988), its economy was in free-fall with high inflation, unemployment, and shortages of goods (Hume, 1994; Souresrafil, 1989). In addition to these conditions, Iran also feared the possibility of a looming catastrophe in which Iraq would use the air superiority it enjoyed in 1988 to attack Iranian cities with chemical weapons (Zartman, 1991).

Put together, these conditions created a mutually hurting stalemate for both Iran and Iraq, coupled with fears that circumstances would grow worse, precisely the conditions that Zartman (2000) sees as most decisive in creating ripeness for successful conflict management. As a result, Iran accepted the terms of UN Resolution 598, establishing a cease-fire between Iran and Iraq. What is distinct about the development of ripeness during the Iran–Iraq War is that its development required changes in the beliefs of only one side in the conflict. After seeing its expectations of a quick, decisive victory over Iran dashed early on, the Iraqi government stated its willingness to accept terms similar to those put in place by UN 598 several years before the end of the conflict. However, it was only when developments on the battlefield and fears about the future convinced Iran that establishing a cease-fire was preferable to continuing to pay conflict costs in pursuit of punishment of Iraq and its leadership for their aggression in 1980 that ripeness developed for both sides and conflict management efforts became more fruitful.

Outside Intervention and the Development of MHS during the Bosnian War

Similar to the Iran–Iraq War, developments on the battlefield during the Bosnian War increased the willingness of the warring sides to make the concessions needed to reach a settlement and establish a lasting peace. As with the Iran–Iraq War, the Bosnian settlement that was put into place by the Dayton Accords was quite similar to peace proposals that had been offered earlier in the conflict and rejected by one or more of the warring sides. As a result, all of the parties were forced to continue to pay conflict costs for several more years while the number of civilians killed and displaced by the war mounted. Despite these similarities, there were also a number of important differences between the two conflicts that carried important implications for conflict management. Unlike the bilateral Iran–Iraq War, the Bosnian War was a multiparty conflict involving Bosnian Serbs, Serbs, Bosnian Croats, Croats, Bosniaks, as well as outside parties that intervened in the conflict. Although the development of a mutually hurting stalemate and the sense of a precipice played a key role in establishing peace in both conflicts, the influence of outside powers played a much more decisive role in establishing those conditions in the Bosnian conflict.

The breakup of Yugoslavia following the end of the Cold War created a series of conflicts that threatened wider conflict in the region. After Slovenia and Croatia declared independence from Yugoslavia in 1991, Bosnia faced a choice between remaining in a Yugoslavia dominated by Serbs or declaring independence and raising fears of domination by Bosnian Muslims among Bosnian Serbs and Bosnian Croats (Cousens and Cater, 2001). Such fears were particularly acute in Bosnia because of its ethnic make-up. Not only did Bosnia have large Serb and Croat minorities, comprising 31% and 17% of the total population respectively, but there was a great deal of geographic intermingling among them. In March 1992, Bosnia held a referendum on independence. Boycotted by Bosnian Serbs who wanted to remain as a constituent part of Yugoslavia, the referendum was supported by 99% of voters (Paris, 2004). Upon passage of the referendum, fighting among Bosnia's ethnic groups ensued almost immediately, escalating quickly to a full civil war.

At the outset of the conflict, the Bosnian government found itself confronting not only Bosnian Serbs that sought to cleanse territory held by them of non-Serbs who were backed by support from the Serbian government in Belgrade, but also Bosnian Croats who sought to seize Croatian-dominated territory in central and southern Bosnia (Cousens and Cater, 2001; Paris, 2004). In response to the conflict, the United Nations dispatched peacekeepers (UNPROFOR) to Bosnia in June 1992 with a mandate to provide humanitarian relief to civilians impacted by the conflict. The mandate for this mission would change over time as the conflict intensified and its impact upon civilians grew. Ultimately, in 1993 UNPROFOR's mandate was expanded to include the protection of safe areas in Srebrenica, Bihac, Sarajevo, Gorazde, Zepla, and Tuzla.

Efforts to settle the Bosnian conflict made little headway during this period. In January 1993, the international community proposed the Vance–Owen peace plan, which called for the division of Bosnia into ten provinces, three for each ethnic community and a UN-supervised Sarajevo province, which was rejected by Bosnian Serbs (Rogel, 2004). Bosnian Muslims rejected the follow-up Owen–Stoltenberg plan offered in July 1993, which called for the establishment of a Bosnian confederation comprised of Muslim, Croat, and Serb units. Beyond the inherent complexity of the conflict, efforts seeking to manage the Bosnian War were also challenged by disagreements among policy makers over whether the conflict was primarily a consequence of Serbian aggression against the Bosnian government or the result of the sharp ethnic divisions of Bosnia, with no one group primarily to blame for the violence (Cousens and Cater, 2001; Goldstein and Pevehouse, 1997). This lack of clarity on the root causes of the conflict, coupled with the refusal of Bosniaks to submit to any agreement that gave up territory ethnically cleansed by Serbs and the lack of incentives for Bosnian Serbs to negotiate while achieving success on the battlefield, undermined efforts to mediate the conflict (Paris, 2004).

Change in the dynamics of the conflict began in 1994 with the start of NATO air involvement in Bosnia. Initially, NATO action was confined to patrolling the UN-sanctioned no-fly zone in Bosnia while providing limited ground support for UN peacekeepers. NATO's role, however, expanded significantly in late 1995 following a series of Serbian attacks on civilians. In July 1995, Bosnian Serb forces attacked the UN safe area in Srebrenica, executing thousands of Muslim men and boys. In August 1995, Bosnian Serb forces fired mortar shells on Sarajevo's Markale, killing thirty-seven people and wounding ninety. This followed an earlier February 1994 Bosnian Serb shelling of the same location that killed over a hundred civilians. These attacks contributed to a more aggressive NATO stance in Bosnia, with NATO forces beginning sustained airstrikes against Bosnian Serb targets at the end of August 1995. NATO forces attacked the Bosnian Serb anti-aircraft network, military depots, artillery positions, ammunition factories, and military positions over an eleven-day period.

The combination of NATO strikes against Bosnian Serb

targets and Bosnian Serb defeats on the battlefield contributed to the development of a hurting stalemate that was decisive in getting the warring parties to the negotiating table and forcing them to make the concessions necessary to produce a settlement. In addition to the effects of NATO bombing, Croatian military advances on the ground put more pressure on the Bosnian Serbs and their Serbian supporters. By the latter part of 1995, the tide on the ground had swung against the Serbs such that they had gone from enjoying a significant military advantage to losing most of their holdings of Croatian territory and faced the real possibility of losing key Bosnian Serb territory in Banja Luka and in western Republika Srpska (Cousens and Cater, 2001). At the same time, Bosniak forces were helped by efforts to "level the battlefield" by removing the outside arms embargo, and they increased offensives against Bosnian Serb forces (Sremac, 1999). This combination of NATO bombing, Croatian military advances, and Bosniak offensives contributed to the development of a mutually hurting stalemate (Cousens and Cater, 2001; Zartman, 2001). The mutually hurting stalemate was effective in promoting settlement among the parties because it created both a temporary setback that was painful and worrisome for the Bosnian Serbs and a temporary advance for the Croats and Bosniaks that could not be held permanently (Zartman, 2001). As a result, each side had an incentive to get to the bargaining table and negotiate a settlement.

The role that an outside power played in encouraging the development of and exploiting the opportunities presented by a mutually hurting stalemate is a unique feature of the Bosnian War. During 1995, mediation, military, and humanitarian efforts became better coordinated by NATO and the United Nations (Cousens and Cater, 2001). Because he was willing and able to employ air-strikes against the Serbs to force them to the negotiating table, US envoy Richard

Holbrooke enjoyed substantial leverage over both Serbian and Bosnian Serb alternatives to a negotiated agreement (Curran et al., 2004). Holbrooke was able to maximize pressure on the Serbs by both encouraging Bosniak and Croat military advances against Serbian positions and using NATO air-strikes to push the Bosnian Serbs and their Serbian allies to the bargaining table. In August 1995, Holbrooke, in meeting with continued Serb intransigence, stated: "If this peace process does not get dramatically moving in the next week or two, the consequences will be very adverse to the Serbian goals" (quoted in Curran et al., 2004: 519). In this respect, the Bosnian War ended with a "coerced compromise" in which outside military pressure significantly altered the military situation on the ground and encouraged agreement between the parties (Cousens and Cater, 2001).

The end result of the pressure applied by NATO was the occurrence of talks in Geneva in September 1995 between the warring sides that created a framework for agreement. These talks were followed by the November 1995 talks at Wright-Patterson Air Force Base just outside Dayton, Ohio, yielding a comprehensive settlement among all of the parties involved in the conflict. This settlement established a cease-fire among the sides, a Bosnia divided into two co-equal parts, the Bosniak and Croat Federation of Bosnia and Herzegovina and the Bosnian Serb Republika Srpksa, and the creation of a three-member presidency with a representative of each ethnic group holding office. As was the case in the Iran–Iraq War, many of the terms of settlement established at Dayton were similar to proposals made years earlier as part of the 1992 Cutilero plan and the 1993 Owen–Stoltenberg plan (Hampson, 2006). Nevertheless, it took years of fighting, death, and destruction to compel the parties to reach a settlement that might have otherwise been achieved years earlier.

CHAPTER FIVE

The Connections and Consequences of Individual Mediation Efforts

In the previous chapters, and consistent with most research on the subject, we generally treated individual mediation efforts as independent of one another and indeed distinct from other conflict management efforts. Yet we know that successive mediation attempts are likely related to one another, if only because the actors who undertake them are aware of the successes or failures of previous efforts. Because many successive mediation efforts are carried out by the same third party, it is implausible to assume that prior efforts are ignored in later mediation attempts. Instead, these linked mediation efforts can be part of a broader peace process that extends across a series of connected mediation initiatives, meetings, proposals, and agreements. In addition, we recognize that mediation efforts are not the only conflict management approach available to the international community, and Chapter 1 outlined some of the similarities and differences between mediation and those other approaches. Yet we know little about how those efforts go together. Accordingly, the first section of this chapter looks at how mediation attempts are sequenced in relation to each other as well as with respect to other conflict management approaches. We also consider how the short-term success of some mediation efforts impacts the long-term goals of peaceful resolution.

Since mediation efforts are rarely isolated from other conflict management approaches, it is important to understand how they interact with one another in promoting the common goals of conflict management and conflict resolution. Although there are multiple combinations of approaches, we focus on one of the most prominent for illustrative purposes: the reciprocal influence of mediation efforts and peacekeeping operations. In the middle section of the chapter, we look at how peacekeeping operations influence the effectiveness of mediation in getting disputants to the table and in facilitating settlements. This helps illuminate the short versus long connection of success in conflict management. A case study of the Cyprus conflict at the end of this chapter illustrates many of these connections.

The previous chapter concentrated on success in mediation, focusing primarily on getting disputants to the table and achieving a settlement agreement. Yet mediation success might also be measured according to the durability of the settlement, or how long it lasts before it breaks down and violence is renewed. Thus, the third section of this chapter focuses on the factors affecting settlement durability, directly and otherwise associated with mediation efforts.

Mediation in Sequence

Individual mediation attempts do not occur in isolation, but are part of a complex set of conflict management approaches including other simultaneous and sequential mediation efforts. From the perspective of individual conflicts, the probability that a mediation attempt will be followed up by another attempt is 92%, indicating that the vast majority of conflicts remain unsettled after the first mediation effort and require a string of multiple mediation efforts for settlement. Quite often, these successive attempts are carried out by the same mediator. Indeed, such attempts occur 34% of the time, as in the case of the Falklands War when UN Secretary-General Perez de Cueller mediated between Britain and Argentina four times during May 1982. Other repeat mediation efforts by the same mediator occur over a longer time frame, such as Perez de Cueller's thirteen mediation efforts of the Iran–Iraq War from 1985 to 1991. This initially might seem counter-intuitive in that the parties are willing to accept the same actor performing additional mediation when previous efforts were less than fully successful; if a complete settlement occurred, there would be no need for further negotiations. Yet some progress might have taken place and thus it makes sense to have the same mediator build on partial settlements and agreements from the past. Still, even when failure occurred, the parties might have clarified issues in dispute, agreed to future deliberations, and established trust and a working relationship with the same mediator. In those events, staying with the same mediator might portend future success.

We see evidence of this pattern among post-World War II conflicts in the data. For those conflicts in which a mediator has previously failed to secure an agreement, nearly 31% of subsequent mediation efforts by that same mediator result in a partial or full agreement while 61% of subsequent efforts fail. A history of failed mediation is evidence that a conflict is more difficult to successfully manage than an average dispute, but follow-up mediation by the same mediator can improve the prospects for its success. This underscores the importance played by the development of a relationship between third party and disputants. US Ambassador Chester Crocker's mediation efforts during the Namibian independence conflict are a good example of success after earlier failure. Following failed mediation efforts in April 1981 and June 1988, Crocker's team successfully brokered a cease-fire in July 1988 and a settlement to the conflict in October 1988.

Because mediation efforts build upon one another, there might be interconnections between what they achieve in the short term versus what impact they have on the long-term relationship between enemies. Greig (2001) has demonstrated that the conditions for short-term success are not the same as those that promote long-term success. Thus, one cannot assume that the achievement of limited success in the immediate term will necessarily lead to long-term progress in future mediation attempts. For example, the achievement of a cease-fire agreement will not automatically translate into a settlement that resolves the underlying disputed issues. Numerous cease-fires between the Israelis and the Palestinians have not produced a comprehensive peace settlement even as they have periodically reduced the number of bombings and retaliatory raids. Mediation efforts that produce a cease-fire do not significantly increase the likelihood of a full agreement in subsequent mediation efforts by either the same mediator or a different one. Only 6% of mediation efforts following a mediated cease-fire result in a full settlement to the conflict.

Greig (2001) makes the distinction between short-term success, often indicated by a limited agreement between the parties, and long-term success. Although agreement success may be achieved, the impact of the mediation effort upon the broader relationship between the disputants remains to be decided. A mediated agreement can be put in place, only to be subsequently broken without more profoundly impacting the relationship between disputants. Longer-term success occurs when a mediation effort positively improves the relationship between disputing states by reducing their conflictual behavior after mediation. A mediation effort that reduces the frequency of future conflict between disputants has achieved behavioral success because it has positively improved the behavior of the disputants after the mediation.

Among the most difficult contexts in which to change conflict behavior are enduring rivalries (Diehl and Goertz,

2000; Colaresi et al., 2008), the long-standing militarized competitions between the same pairs of states, such as India and Pakistan. In these cases, enemies lock in their hostile behaviors and, although not all such conflicts escalate to war, they are characterized by frequent military crises and confrontations that are difficult to terminate in the absence of a dramatic shock or change in the political environment. Enduring rivalries attract a disproportionate share of mediation efforts, almost double the rate of interstate conflicts occurring in non-rivalry contexts. This is not surprising in that these competitions are the most dangerous and have the greatest implications for the international system. Yet mediation's impact on the long-term dynamics of those rivalries has been limited. Mediation does not appear to diminish the severity (including the prospects for full-scale war) of future conflict in enduring rivalries, although it has a modest effect in delaying the onset of that next conflict (Bercovitch et. al., 1997; Diehl and Goertz, 2000). Thus, short-term progress in mediation might provide false hope for dealing with threats to international peace and security, especially the most intractable conflicts.

The interconnection of individual mediation attempts in conflict management is not confined to other mediation initiatives. Mediation is also linked to other approaches including verbal actions (e.g. statements urging an end to the fighting, resolutions from international organizations urging peaceful settlements), legal efforts, peace operations, and others. Owsiak (2011) refers to the sequencing of these different approaches, including mediation, as conflict management "trajectories." In interstate conflicts, third parties, whether the same actors or not, tend to reuse strategies at the lower end of the cost scale in successive interventions, with verbal strategies and mediation being the most prominent examples. Following a mediation attempt, actors are most likely (slightly over 50% of the time) to adopt a verbal strategy, such as calling for a cease-fire or denouncing violence that might be occurring. Another mediation attempt is likely about one third of the time, but third parties rarely adopt more costly strategies (e.g. economic sanctions) following a decision to mediate. The success of the previous mediation has some effect on the follow-up conflict management effort, with successful mediations making another mediation attempt the most likely outcome, and unsuccessful attempts only slightly decreasing the probability of another mediation effort. In general, whatever the conflict management approaches, Owsiak (2011) finds that verbal strategies and mediation are by far the modal actions in follow-up efforts. Thus, mediation attempts occur frequently following a variety of other conflict management techniques, including other mediation efforts.

Mediation and Peacekeeping

Mediation efforts have interaction effects with other conflict management approaches and thus in this section we examine their interconnection with one of the most visible actions taken by the international community to manage conflict: peacekeeping. Peacekeeping has become an increasingly prominent tool used by the international community to promote conflict management and resolution. Indeed, in the history of the United Nations, over three fourths of its peacekeeping operations have been initiated since 1988. Many of the operations have been put in place following a cease-fire, but prior to a peace agreement. Indeed, mediation might have facilitated such a halt in the fighting. Yet, once in place, does peacekeeping enhance the prospects for gaining a settlement between protagonists? There are competing views – optimistic and pessimistic – of how peacekeepers affect mediation and other negotiation efforts.

The Optimistic View

UN Secretary-General Boutros-Ghali has argued that peacekeeping "expands the possibilities for ... the making of peace" (Boutros-Ghali, 1995: 45). Indeed, one of the key factors thought to affect the success of mediation and negotiation attempts is the level of conflict between the disputants at the time of those efforts. Most peacekeeping operations have as one of their primary (or only) purposes to limit armed conflict. If they are successful in preventing the renewal of hostilities (i.e., actually keep the peace), peacekeeping operations create an environment in which the disputants are more likely to be open to diplomatic initiatives and to settle their differences. Intense conflict between disputants is thought to undermine the prospects for mediation success. By implication then, factors that lessen the intensity of that conflict contribute to peacemaking triumphs.

There are several theoretical rationales why intense conflict is deleterious to mediation and negotiation, and why a cease-fire promotes the conditions under which mediators can facilitate an agreement between the opposing sides. First, a cooling-off period, evidenced by a cease-fire, can lessen hostilities and build some trust between the protagonists. In times of armed conflict, leaders and domestic audiences become habituated to the conflict. They become psychologically committed to the conflict, and some segments of the population profit politically and economically from the fighting (Crocker et al., 2004). Before diplomatic efforts can be successful, this process must be broken or interrupted, something with which peacekeepers can assist by maintaining a cease-fire.

Second, intense conflict puts domestic political constraints on leaders who might otherwise be inclined to sign a peace agreement. Negotiating with the enemy may have significant political costs during active hostilities. Calls for cease-fires or pauses in bombing attacks in order to promote negotiations and diplomatic efforts are consistent with this underlying logic. Of course, this presumes that hostilities harden bargaining positions and attitudes, rather than leading to concessions by parties suffering significant costs.

Third, and from a somewhat different vantage point, active conflict leads decision-makers to concentrate on the ongoing hostilities (a short-term concern), and therefore they will not place settlement issues (a longer-term concern) high on their agendas. That is, during heightened armed conflict, political and diplomatic attention will be devoted to the conduct of the fighting and at best to short-range conflict management issues such as securing a cease-fire.

Fourth, that the international community has provided peacekeepers may signal to the disputants the willingness of the international community to commit additional resources to any settlement that would follow such a deployment.

Traditional peacekeeping operations are most often put in place after a cease-fire has been achieved. The expectation of the optimists therefore would be that conflict settlements would be more likely after the imposition of those forces relative to other scenarios; this is essentially the assumption underlying Secretary-General Boutros-Ghali's proposals (Boutros-Ghali, 1995). Yet an important caveat to this expectation is that diplomacy will fail if peacekeepers do not keep the peace; that is, the positive spin-off effects of peacekeeping are predicated on cease-fires holding. The first three logics above suggest that parties would be more willing to negotiate in the presence of peacekeeping, as well as more successful in negotiating efforts. The final logic, based on signaling international commitment, is suggestive of more frequent mediation attempts by members of the global community, including by states and international organizations. Thus, peacekeeping should be associated with more frequent mediation and negotiation attempts as well as promoting a greater success rate when they do occur.

The Pessimistic View

At the other end of the spectrum are theoretical logics positing a negative effect of peacekeeping operations on peacemaking initiatives. There are two primary positions, those based on rational choice and on hurting stalemates, respectively. Although they differ in a number of ways, both rely on peacekeeping's achievement of a cease-fire and share the same pessimistic prediction that peacekeeping will make conflict resolution efforts less successful.

In some rational choice conceptions, war and other militarized competitions are essentially information problems. War begins because there is some uncertainty about the outcome of a confrontation between disputants. Under conditions of perfect information, disputants would *ex ante* come to an agreement, and therefore not incur the costs of competition. Cetinyan (2002), for example, argues that bargaining breakdown in ethnic conflicts occurs because of the problems of information and commitments, not capability differences between the parties. Fighting provides each side with information about capabilities and resolve such that they can predict likely outcomes of future confrontations; war ends when the two sides have clear information about those outcomes (Fearon, 1995). Peacekeeping interrupts this information flow and thereby leaves some uncertainty as to which side might prevail if armed hostilities would resume. Thus, peacekeepers prevent the transmission of information necessary for the parties to settle.

Rational choice theorists might predict that the introduction of peacekeeping forces limits the effectiveness of diplomatic efforts, given that uncertainty still exists about future outcomes. Thus, peacekeeping should be negatively associated with diplomatic success. Peacekeeping operations that fail in maintaining cease-fires therefore may produce positive spillover effects on mediation and negotiation efforts; fighting renews the flow of information about capabilities and resolve to the participants.

Peacekeeping should not necessarily be an absolute barrier to diplomatic settlement according to the rational choice perspective. Mediators may be able to provide necessary information to the participants, if those third parties possess such information and are regarded as credible by the disputants (Smith and Stam, 2003). Thus, one might expect that the negative relationship between peacekeeping and peacemaking would be more muted for mediation than for negotiation, the latter of which only involves the primary parties. Yet, even for mediation, disputants must agree that they can each do better by participating in mediation than by relying upon a unilateral effort to impose a settlement upon one another. To the extent that peacekeeping limits the likelihood that this perception will develop among disputants, it will undermine settlement of the issues between them. Peacekeeping reduces the likelihood of negotiation between the disputants for the same reason it reduces the likelihood of success – because it limits information available to the disputants. This reduction would decrease the willingness of either side to initiate negotiations for fear that this would signal weakness to the opposing side. Conversely, peacekeeping could increase the likelihood of mediation between disputants. Mediation is often proposed by a third party. As a result, accepting the proposal of a third party for mediation does not signal the potential weakness that unilaterally calling for negotiations does. In addition, the presence of peacekeeping forces can provide information about the conflict and prospects for its resolution to third parties, increasing their willingness to intervene diplomatically.

A variation of the pessimistic view, but with the same

conclusion about the deleterious effects of peacekeeping, is rooted in the hurting stalemate concept discussed in the previous chapter (Zartman, 2000). Under such conditions, the disputants will look for a way out of their stalemate and thereby be open to attempts to settle their differences. Peacekeeping operations may lessen the "ripeness" for conflict resolution by diminishing the chances for a hurting stalemate. By limiting armed conflict, peacekeeping may decrease the costs to all sides in the conflict. Thus, without ongoing costs in terms of lives or military resources, disputants may harden their bargaining positions and be resistant to diplomatic efforts. Peacekeeping might also lessen the time pressure on the disputants (Diehl, 1994). Peacekeeping operations, *de facto*, have no explicit deadlines and therefore disputants may feel little need to resolve differences immediately, hoping for better terms of settlement later. Peacekeeping would seem to have effects mostly on the cost side of the hurting stalemate equation. A cease-fire successfully monitored by peacekeepers might at first glance seem to facilitate a stalemate; yet this depends significantly on which side (if either) benefits from a freezing of the status quo.

Empirical Findings and the Peacekeeping–Peacemaking Dilemma

The results of the analyses in Greig and Diehl (2005) cast a rather dim light on the ability of peacekeeping forces to assist the conflict resolution process. In enduring rivalries, the presence of peacekeeping forces reduced the occurrence of mediation and negotiation attempts as well as diminished the prospects for their success when they did actually take place, at least with respect to achieving a broad peace agreement. The effects with respect to civil wars were not as harmful, but neither did peacekeeping have the kind of positive impacts it was designed to have. There was virtually no support throughout any of the analyses for the optimistic view that peacekeeping promotes peacemaking. The pessimistic view was supported in most of the analyses. The hurting stalemate model and rational choice models were confirmed in that they predicted fewer settlements in the presence of peacekeeping. The results tended to support the hurting stalemate model in that costs had an important influence on diplomatic initiatives and successful outcomes. The rational choice logic was prescient in anticipating stronger negative effects on negotiation success than mediation success. The results are perhaps not strong enough to privilege one model over the other. Yet it may be that a combined model might provide the best explanatory combination. Most easily accommodated would be factoring in the cost elements of the hurting stalemate model into the rational choice approach. The stalemate element is certainly consistent with the rational choice notion of information about future outcomes, and the cost elements permit states to opt out of civil wars and rivalry, which are admittedly expensive ways to gain additional information.

Although a hybrid explanation is promising, a remaining empirical puzzle comes from the finding that when peacekeepers failed to keep the peace (that is, peacekeeping forces on the ground did not prevent severe violence), third parties and disputants alike made fewer efforts at peacemaking. Having a peacekeeping operation that fails to keep the peace is worse than continuing the fighting with no peacekeeping deployment. If anything, this is consistent with a strongly pessimistic view of peacekeeping and peacemaking, although it does not fit with either of the pessimist logics discussed above.

The findings suggest that policy makers confronted with an ongoing conflict face a difficult dilemma. On one hand, there are powerful political, strategic, and moral reasons for deploying a peacekeeping force in conflicts marked by mounting bloodshed. Cases of genocide or recurring warfare may be so extreme that they demand peacekeeping forces in order to separate the combatants and prevent the renewal of fighting. Indeed, the prospect of peacekeeping deployment may be the only way to get the protagonists to agree to a cease-fire in the first place. Once deployed, peacekeeping forces may be the best mechanism for stabilizing the situation. Yet, the intervention of peacekeepers may not only represent just a temporary solution to the fighting, but may also hinder mediation efforts aimed at resolving the issues in enduring rivalries that created the conflict in the first place. This paradox works to create situations such as in the Golan Heights (also Cyprus – see below) in which peacekeepers are deployed for decades, but little movement toward agreement or settlement occurs. Nevertheless, this is not to diminish the positive effects that flow from ending bloodshed and allowing the local population to live as normal lives as possible. If peacekeepers fail to keep the peace effectively, however, as has been the case in southern Lebanon and in the Congo, then conflict resolution efforts by third parties or the disputants themselves may dry up. In those cases, not only has conflict resolution been negatively impacted, but there is not even the benefit of saving lives and promoting stability in the area, the primary purpose of most peacekeeping deployments.

The other horn of the dilemma is present if decision-makers choose to defer the deployment of peacekeeping forces until after a peace agreement. In one sense, it may be advantageous in the long term for conflict to continue to occur unabated without the intervention of peacekeepers in order to allow the conflict to progress to a stage in which the disputants become more amenable to settlement (see Luttwak 2001, for example). Yet, such a hands-off approach is likely to be unpalatable in the most extreme cases of conflict and may carry the risk of conflict expansion, effectively compelling third parties to intervene militarily. Furthermore, decision-makers may wait for a peace agreement that never comes, as there is no guarantee that the conditions for ending an enduring rivalry or civil war will ever be manifest, at least not for many years. At minimum, the results of this study suggest the need for third parties to be judicious in their use of peacekeeping, balancing the immediate need to limit conflict with the long-term goal of producing a settlement.

Although the empirical results provide a bleak outlook on the relationship between peacekeeping and mediation/ negotiation success, there remain other areas in which peacekeeping operations enhance efforts at conflict resolution. It may be that the *prospect* of peacekeeping, rather than the actual presence of peacekeeping forces, promotes mediation and negotiation success. Disputants may be willing to commit to an agreement if they know that peacekeepers will be there afterward to guarantee the settlement. By acting as guarantors of agreements, peacekeepers may serve to lessen the possibility of renewed fighting when disputes over the implementation of agreements arise. In addition, the prospect of peacekeeping may positively influence the content of agreements reached. Protagonists may be more willing to commit to more detailed settlement provisions and those which address a broader range of disputed issues if some guarantees, facilitated by peacekeepers, exist such that provisions will be implemented with full compliance. These are aspects that are discussed in the next section with respect to settlement durability.

The Durability of Settlements

Regardless of its scope, achieving an agreement between warring parts is quite an accomplishment for a mediator. Yet the ultimate value of an agreement is manifest only if the settlement is actually implemented and endures for a significant period of time. Absent this, the disputants and third parties might find themselves returning to the second phase of conflict and the need to stop the fighting and negotiate a settlement all over again. For example, the Bicesse agreement (mediated by Portugal) to end the violence between rival factions and hold elections in Angola in 1991 broke down quickly and the country was plunged back into civil war.

Much depends on how one defines conflict management success and what constitutes a breakdown of settlement. Nevertheless, the most common measure of conflict management success is the time elapsed from the signing of a peace agreement to the onset of any new violent conflict. By this standard, the durability of most conflict management outcomes is remarkably short. Working with the same data that we have used throughout this book, more than a third of agreements between disputants last less than eight weeks (Gartner and Bercovitch, 2006; Gartner and Melin, 2009). Of course, a number of these agreements include only a commitment to honor a cease-fire and therefore do not resolve the underlying sources of contention. Not surprisingly, such agreements tend to break down as was frequently the case during the civil war in Bosnia when more than half lasted one week or less.

Given these figures, it might be tempting to dismiss mediated agreements as worth little more than the paper on which they are printed and signed. Yet, mediators, and third parties in general, become involved in those conflicts that are among the most intractable and often the most violent. Accordingly, it is perhaps not surprising that the post-settlement failure rate is so high just as the recovery rate for patients with advanced cancer is so low. As we note below, many of the factors that are associated with the durability of peace settlements are largely outside the control of mediators.

Hartzell and Yuen (2012) provide an overview of the factors associated with the durability of peace settlements involving a wide range of conflicts and including different kinds of third-party intervention (or not). Scholarship is often characterized by conflicting findings, but it is clear that many of the factors thought to be important for durable peace are related to the conflict itself and not necessarily to the attributes of conflict management efforts. Some of the factors relate to the kinds of conflict or the issues in dispute between the protagonists. There is a debate in the literature over whether ethnic conflict is more prone to recurrence than other conflict (Fortna, 2008; Cederman et. al., 2010). There is some consensus, however, that disputes over territory are more likely to reignite (Grieco, 2001), mirroring the general findings in studies of war onset that indicate that territorial conflict is more prone to escalation. Of course, there are limits (if not absolute limits) to the degree to which mediators can reframe conflict issues away from those that tend to undermine any settlements.

The severity of conflict is also associated with the durability of peace (Mattes and Savun, 2010). Longer conflicts might produce more durable peace, at least in civil wars, as protracted conflicts are better able to convey information about future behavior based on past interactions. Yet more intense conflicts, in the form of high death tolls over short periods, might prompt greater hostility and sow the seeds for the breakdown of any settlement. Neveretheless, Hartzell and Yuen (2012) report that this effect is more common in civil wars than in interstate wars, the latter actually being less inclined to reerupt in the future. Again, mediators can do little to manipulate these conditions. They might be able to choose the timing of their intervention, but this doesn't guarantee success. As noted with the peacekeeping analysis above, however, an early intervention might have stopped the bloodshed but undermined a durable peace; a later intervention might produce a more durable outcome, but at the cost of many lives and property damage.

Beyond the characteristics of the conflict, the attributes of the disputants have also been found to influence whether an agreement will hold in the long run or not. There are some divergent findings on exactly what those attributes might be, and their effects might vary across the intra versus interstate context of the dispute. For example, pairs of democratic states have longer-lasting settlements than states with other regime type configurations (Quackenbush and Venteicher, 2008); it is not clear whether democracy is equally advantageous as a pacifying condition in civil wars. Research is decidedly mixed on whether favorable economic conditions after a war promote long-term peace or not (Collier et al., 2008; Morey, 2009). The relative power distribution between the combatants might also affect the onset (or not) of future conflict. Regardless, mediators cannot change these conditions, and it is difficult to structure agreements that would alter their configuration as other processes condition their presence as well as any future changes.

The above discussion might imply that mediators have little influence over the long-term stability of an agreement. With respect to certain key factors, this is an accurate assessment. Nevertheless, the durability of peace agreements is also affected by how conflict ends and what elements are contained in the agreements, conditions over which mediation has some impact.

Conflicts can end through many different processes and thus it is possible to compare those in which negotiated agreements (including those achieved through mediation) occurred with other outcomes. There is a preponderance of scholarly findings that outright victories by one side produce the most stable, if not the most just, peace (Grieco, 2001). That is, allowing a war to continue to its natural outcome leads to longer peace periods thereafter; a mediated agreement that produces less than a full victory interferes with the conflict resolution process and results in a less durable peace. Nevertheless, settlements negotiated between the parties, often involving mediation, are more durable that other referent categories of conflict outcomes (Hensel, 1994). Specifically, stalemate and other inconclusive outcomes are generators of future conflict (Goertz et al., 2005), and mediated agreements are certainly superior to those. Of course, as noted above, mediators often intervene in the most difficult conflicts, so it is not necessarily an even playing field to make comparisons across approaches, and indeed the durability of mediated settlements looks better in light of this fact.

Mediators might produce better agreements or outcomes in general, and therefore ones likely to endure, by their participation in the process. This is related to the ability of mediators to secure an agreement, which has spillover effects in the long run. First, mediators can provide valuable information and suggested settlement conditions that the parties would otherwise not consider themselves, as well as other approaches (e.g. adjudication) that the parties would not or could not generate themselves. In this way, the disputants are better able to select an optimal or near-optimal outcome; the result is that the parties are more likely to be more satisfied and less inclined to seek renegotiation or a return to the battlefield in order to get a better deal. Similarly, mediators can provide carrots and sticks to the negotiating parties that induce them to come to an agreement; these additional benefits or sanctions in coming to an agreement can increase the incentives for protagonists to adhere to the agreement after it has been signed. Again, these are not tools available in the absence of a third party, and legal proceedings are generally barred from including such additional inducements in their settlements. Nevertheless, Beardsley (2008) suggests that mediators are best able to promote long-term peace when the provision of inducements and sanctions extends beyond the initial agreements and continues well after the settlement document is signed.

In particular, mediators might be able to facilitate the inclusion of certain provisions in the settlement that enhance durability, and third parties can also provide guarantees about the implementation of those provisions. Depending on the provisions of the treaty or agreement, it might last a short time or be enduring. One key consideration is the degree to which the agreement resolves the underlying issues in dispute between the protagonists. Cease-fire agreements are perhaps the easiest to achieve, but also the most vulnerable to breaking down as the degree of consensus among the parties is quite narrow: they only share the interest in stopping the fighting, not necessarily in how to resolve their differences. Partial agreements are more common and represent greater convergence of interests in implementing and complying with any agreement. Full settlements clearly indicate that all major issues have been resolved, but such agreements are the least common outcome among mediated settlements. Other agreement provisions are context-specific in terms of how they influence durability. For example, power-sharing arrangements might be critical for ending a civil war, but do not necessarily lead to a durable peace in the long run (Rothchild, 2002) as contending parties find it difficult to cooperate in the post-war environment.

Mediators have some influence in determining what kind of provisions appear in an agreement. They can strategically limit the scope of negotiations to those issues on which agreement is most likely, hoping to build momentum for future progress; this will result in more limited agreements (e.g. cease-fires) that might not hold in the long run unless they are followed by more far-reaching settlements. Mediators also influence the configuration of agreements by suggesting certain alternatives or crafting the specific details of various alternatives. The extent to which these are wise or effective strategies rests in part with the judgment of the mediator. Nevertheless, the choice of alternatives that ultimately appear in the settlement is made by the disputants based on their joint preferences. Accordingly, they bear some, if not a majority, of the credit (or blame) for when peace agreements last (or do not).

Perhaps the greatest influence that third parties have on agreement durability comes from providing so-called guarantees to the implementation of the agreements. The contributions of mediators and other third parties come from providing solutions to the "credible commitment" problem (Walter, 2002; Fortna, 2004). Parties might have an interest in reaching an agreement with a certain set of provisions, but be reluctant to sign on because they do not trust the other side to keep its word in implementing the agreement. This lack of trust is not surprising given that the two sides likely have endured years of hostility, and perhaps open warfare. One oft-cited example is the provision in many civil war settlements that involves the disarmament of rebel groups. Yet what is to stop a government from reneging on its commitments after the rebel group gives up its weapons? The government could, in theory, refuse to carry out its obligations and/or attack rebel supporters, and do so with impunity. It is also the case that the disputants are uncertain about future conditions that might influence the willingness of their opponent to keep its word; for example, changing power configurations could lead one side to break an agreement or insist on renegotiating the terms when it is in a more advantageous position. The commitment problem is one that will prevent parties from signing on to an agreement (stage 2) and will complicate the implementation of an agreement (stage 3) should a settlement ever be reached.

Mediators can address the credible commitment problem in several ways. First, they can provide suggestions on a range of guarantees that solve the uncertainty or trust problems that make the disputants reluctant to sign on to the agreement or comply thereafter. These might include agreement provisions such as establishing demilitarized zones between the warring states, as for example the demilitarization of the Sinai as part of the peace agreement between Israel and Egypt. Mediators, or the entities that they represent, might also directly provide those guarantees. These could come in the form of peace operations that monitor cease-fires, disarmament provisions in the settlement agreement, or monitoring of democratic elections; these have proven effective in lengthening the elapsed time to the next conflict or even ensuring "permanent" peace (Fortna, 2008). For example, UN personnel supervised foreign troop withdrawal and subsequent elections in Namibia, key elements in securing the agreement of South Africa and local political actors as Namibia achieved its independence. Other guarantees might include aid to the participants to assist in implementation or promised further mediation efforts in the event that disputes arise in the final stage. In these ways, mediators can enhance how long a settlement lasts and preclude reversion to earlier conflict stages.

The Case of Cyprus

The conflict over Cyprus provides a good illustration of interconnected mediation attempts to control violence as well as the intersection of diplomatic initiatives and peacekeeping operations. Cyprus had long experienced turmoil between the Greek and Turkish communities who shared the island. Colonial rule under the British managed to keep the lid on the worst of that conflict. Still, during a 1956 crisis in which a rebel group sought unification with Greece, the British dispatched Member of Parliament Francis Noel-Baker to mediate between the island's governor and the guerilla force leader. The failure of those efforts was only the first of many that tried to craft a final settlement to disagreements there.

Britain, Turkey, and Greece signed the London and Zurich agreements (1959) that laid out the constitution of the soon-to-be independent Cyprus. Provisions included power-sharing arrangements between the Greek and Turkish communities, not unlike the arrangements in Lebanon for so many years. The hope was that this would maintain peace on the island for the foreseeable future. Such arrangements did not prove durable as disagreements between the Greek and Turkish residents over the administration of the island flared quickly. A Greek proposal to institute a majority-rule system of government, which would favor the Greeks who outnumbered the Turks by almost four to one, intensified the enmity. In December 1963, fighting broke out between the communities, and there was a threat that Greece and, in particular, Turkey would intervene. Diplomatic efforts by the international community were triggered by this prospect, a pattern of intervention only in the face of crises that would be repeated over the years.

In response to the crisis, the United Nations authorized the creation of a peacekeeping operation, the United Nations Force in Cyprus (UNFICYP), in March 1964. The mandate of the operation was to prevent a recurrence of fighting, restore law and order in the area, and promote a return to normality on the island. The specific tasks included insuring freedom of movement between the ethnic communities and facilitating the evacuation and dismantling of fortified positions by Greek and Turkish Cypriots. UNFICYP forces also manned roadblocks for inspections, investigated incidents, and coordinated actions with the Cypriot police.

The UN resolution that created UNFICYP also included provisions for a UN mediator whose tasks included promoting a settlement between the disputing parties. In addition, UN Secretary-General U Thant appointed a special representative to negotiate on behalf of the UN (Higgins, 1981). The operation went well for UNFICYP during the initial months of deployment. Yet the peace was broken in August 1964 when fighting started in one sector and the Turkish air force was sent to the area. US mediation, working with the UN and including former Secretary of State Dean Acheson, made little progress. Another cease-fire was arranged under the authority of the UNFICYP commander. In the following months, the UN mediator (Galo Plaza of Ecuador) tried to lay the groundwork for a future settlement. He released a report in early 1965 that summarized the issue of positions of the various sides and laid out some possible settlement terms that fell between the extreme and preferred positions of the Greeks and the Turks. Although the governments of Greece and Cyprus accepted the report, Turkey did not. Turkey's unwillingness to work with the mediator led to his resignation, and the Secretary-General decided not to appoint a replacement, preferring instead to rely on the good offices of his special representative.

Intermittent diplomatic efforts continued, but less frequently until another round of violence in 1967. Again the United Nations not only succeeded in reestablishing a cease-fire but also persuaded each side to withdraw its non-indigenous military personnel – that is, soldiers and civilians from Greece and Turkey aiding each side. There were a series of inter-communal talks during the 1967–1974 period, often coordinated by the UN special representative. Although little or no progress was made in promoting a full settlement, there was actually a decline in violent incidents during this period. Sambanis (1999) attributes the latter to a side effect of the negotiations. Thus, mediation might have assisted the peacekeeping force in accomplishing its mission of limiting violence, even if the peacekeeping operation did not help mediation facilitate diplomatic progress.

The next major turning point in the conflict and mediation efforts occurred in the summer of 1974 (see Ertekun, 1984).

The Cyprus government was the victim of a *coup d'etat*, and leaders of the coup wanted to unify the island with Greece and requested assistance from that state. Meanwhile, Turkey did not intend to stand by and permit this outcome; the Turkish government was also alarmed by reports of human rights violations committed against Turkish Cypriots. Turkish forces invaded the island, occupying the northern portion of Cyprus. James Callaghan, Foreign Minister of the former colonial power United Kingdom, facilitated an interim agreement with the Greek and Turkish foreign ministers, but the agreement was not implemented. UN representatives from the peace operation and UN headquarters became involved and helped arrange another cease-fire and some minor agreements on humanitarian issues. Subsequent talks in Vienna involved no fewer than four mediation attempts by the UN Secretary-General Kurt Waldheim and led to an agreement on population movements on the island; again, these were never fully implemented. Some of the blame might be given to UNFICYP for failing to assist in the process, and Sambanis (1999) argues that it was the failures of the peace operation prior to 1975, not its successes in limiting violence, that actually hardened the positions of the respective parties and undermined the long-term prospects for settlement.

In the immediate aftermath, UN mediation continued for the rest of the 1970s, with seventeen different mediation attempts mostly by the UN, specifically by high-ranking individuals such as Secretary-General Waldheim, and his special representative Javier Perez de Cuellar, who would eventually succeed Waldheim as UN leader. Again no settlement occurred, even as the situation on the ground stabilized with UNFICYP patrolling the 180-kilometer demilitarized zone established between the Greek and Turkish forces.

The next major crisis in Cyprus was the unilateral declaration of independence by the Turkish Republic of Northern

Cyprus in late 1983. Mediation efforts proliferated thereafter, with fourteen separate mediation attempts by UN Secretary-General Perez de Cuellar alone in the following three years. His successor Boutros-Ghali assumed the mediator role thereafter, but a settlement or any extensive agreements proved elusive. Meanwhile, UNFICYP had its mandate renewed every six months by the UN, a testimony to its effectiveness at limiting violence but also indicative of the great risk of war and the improbability of settlement if the peacekeepers were withdrawn.

The impending entry of Cyprus into the European Union prompted another wave of mediation efforts to settle the disputes between the Greek and Turkish communities as well as between their respective patrons, Greece and Turkey. Continuing the tradition of high-profile mediation by his predecessors, UN Secretary-General Kofi Annan constructed what became known as the Annan Plan, an attempt at a comprehensive resolution of outstanding issues. Over the course of 2002–2004 (the latter the year of the ascension of Cyprus to EU membership), Annan worked with Greek and Turkish community leaders to refine the plan but could not secure their joint agreement. He submitted a final plan in March 2004 and it was subject to public referendum. Turkish Cypriots voted in favor of the plan, while Greek Cypriots opposed it; accordingly the plan failed. Mediation in the Cyprus conflict has been frequent over the last five decades, characterized by repeated interventions of high-profile UN officials. Notably, UN Secretary-Generals have been persistent in their efforts, refusing to stop with initial failures and building on those efforts; the Annan plan is indicative of this pattern. Yet the vast majority of mediation efforts have been failures. Those successes that have occurred have involved very limited agreements, most often cease-fires following flare-ups in the conflict. Many of these have been unsuccessful, with conflict reerupting, although the post-1975 period has been quite stable in terms of only infrequent violent incidents occurring. More than five decades after its independence, however, Cyprus does not have a settlement of its ethnic troubles.

What role has the UNFICYP operation played in the conflict? Except for the 1974 invasion, UNFICYP has been able to head off the most serious armed conflict, despite several disputes or incidents that might easily have escalated to war. Furthermore, the loss of life on all sides has generally been minimal. For most of the period after peacekeeping deployment, and particularly since 1975, the situation has been relatively calm. In this respect, the operation is a success in one of its missions – limiting armed conflict.

An assessment of its role in supplementing mediation efforts and assisting in conflict resolution is considerably less favorable, despite the UN's own website that headlines that the operation is "contributing to a political settlement in Cyprus." Mediation attempts were seemingly driven more by external events (e.g. Turkish invasion, EU membership) rather than by the actions of the peacekeeping force. Indeed, one might argue that key failures in keeping the peace (e.g. 1974) led to more mediation attempts than those that occurred during periods in which there was less violence. Success in mediation efforts also seems largely unrelated to the activities of the peace operation, with all mediations unable to produce a full settlement. James (1989) argues that UNFICYP is a good means of providing a calm stalemate for the two sides, neither of which desires war; indeed, the induced stalemate is preferable to any of the alternatives thus far offered. An analysis of the conflict "narratives" of both the Greek and Turkish communities concludes that each portrays UNFICYP as contributing to that stalemate (Neack and Knudson, 1999). James (1989) further contends that the two sides could easily agree to a series of partial settlements dealing with cease-fire lines

themselves, without need of the UN force. Yet the continuing presence of the UN force obviates the need for the parties
to negotiate on these issues and thereby prevents any cooperation from spilling over to settlements on more contentious
issues. Thus, Cyprus can be said to be a good illustration of
the peacekeeping–peacemaking dilemma noted above.

CHAPTER SIX

Evolving Challenges for International Mediation

International mediation has experienced a number of notable successes, including securing peace agreements in Northern Ireland and Bosnia. Yet we must remember that mediation failure is the modal outcome. Third parties always face an uphill climb when they step into a conflict that the disputants could not resolve themselves and that most often has already involved some violent encounters. Mediators do not possess magic wands that can easily resolve difficult conflicts. Nevertheless, there remains room for improvement even within these parameters. In this concluding chapter, we explore a series of challenges, whose successful management would enhance the success rate of mediators. We also briefly discuss some areas for future research concerning mediation. At the most fundamental level, taking effective mediator action depends on a solid knowledge base on what works and what doesn't and this can best come from systematic research on mediation processes and outcomes.

Challenges for Mediators

Ad Hoc System
International mediation efforts have grown substantially in recent decades, but the structural provisions for mediation have largely remained unchanged; that is, mediation is initiated and conducted largely on an ad hoc basis. There is no international governmental organization devoted exclusively

or primarily to mediation, nor do most foreign ministries have agencies that take on mediation as one of their primary duties. When mediation occurs, it takes place as the need arises and political or organizational heads designate individuals to carry out the diplomatic efforts. This is not to say that the process is disorganized or ignorant of precedent. As actors take part in several mediation attempts over time, they gain experience with this conflict management strategy and rely on procedures and strategies used in the immediate past. Similarly, the same individuals are often called up to mediate new conflicts based on their track records in the past: George Mitchell of the United States was chosen by President Obama to attempt mediation between the Israelis and the Palestinians, in part because of his central role in facilitating the Good Friday Accords that ended most of the conflict in Northern Ireland.

The current ad hoc system of mediation leads to a number of problems. First is that many conflicts remain unmediated as present arrangements rely on volunteers to recognize that a problem exists and then take appropriate action to intervene in the conflict; accordingly 33% of conflicts are ignored by third parties. An institutionalized arrangement at the global level might be better able to detect problems and ensure that those conflicts that need mediation receive it. The establishment of the Mediation Support Unit (MSU) by the United Nations in 2008, an initiative begun by Norway, represents an initial step in this direction. The MSU maintains a standby team of conflict management experts who are available on request to lend support to efforts to manage ongoing conflicts across the international system.

Second, the present system does not necessarily ensure that the right mediators with proper training are matched with the conflict at hand. There is essentially no research on what are the optimal mediator–conflict interfaces, so it is difficult to assess the scope of the problem and how address-ing it might affect the mediation outcomes. Nevertheless, greater professionalization and some coordination across different actors would seem to be a step forward in maxi-mizing the chances that mediation would be successful. Of course, as reviewed in Chapter 4, mediator characteristics are only one of four general components influencing mediation outcomes.

A more institutionalized approach to mediation would probably require the creation of appropriate units or organiza-tions at the global, regional, and national levels. For example, one might consider setting up a special agency under the UN Secretary-General that was charged with mediation and included a collection of respected diplomats as its staff. This would replace the current arrangements of appointing special representatives as the need arises. Such an agency would need to coordinate with member states and regional organizations, as is done now with respect to peacekeeping operations, since one cannot necessarily assume the UN is always the best actor to carry out the mediation. There would also remain the prob-lem of political will in that even with an organization designed to identify conflicts in need of mediation, various parties must still be willing to supply the intermediary, especially if the UN is unsuitable for such tasks as might be the case for any mediation involving Israel.

The largely ad hoc approach to mediation stands in con-trast to the institutionalization of other conflict management approaches, and thus a few precedents exist on which to build. Multiple examples are relevant. International adjudication is regularized in several ways. There are institutions at the global (e.g. International Court of Justice or ICJ) and regional levels (e.g. European Court of Justice) that have formal rules and procedures, including when the bodies have jurisdiction and when parties are obliged to take their disputes to these venues. Recourse to such courts is also stipulated in treaties that bind states to go to ICJ when signing the Genocide Convention or the dispute resolution forum when joining the World Trade Organization. International commercial arbitration is the primary mechanism for resolving disputes between multinational corporations and others, and this process is a well-established part of transnational contracts and is conducted under the auspices of organizations such as the International Chamber of Commerce.

Peacekeeping missions also began as largely ad hoc operations, with forces and supplies assembled as conflicts arose and organizations authorized peacekeeping operations. To some extent this still occurs. Yet the United Nations and many other regional organizations, such as the African Union and the European Union, have developed specific units devoted to peace operations. These efforts now include bureaucratic support, training protocols, and other regularized procedures for carrying out operations; the same is true of many national militaries who organize peace operations with personnel, logistics, and supplies.

Beyond other conflict management approaches, mediation is institutionalized in some cases at the national level. For example, the Federal Mediation and Conciliation Service is an independent US government agency that provides services to public and private groups across the country. Its personnel include experts in mediation who have extensive training and experience in mediation activities. Other states promote the use of mediation to manage global trouble spots by establishing and supporting government–NGO linkages. Norway's Foreign Ministry, for example, works with a variety of NGOs interested in conflict management. The most famous example of this is Fafo, the Oslo-based research foundation that was the linchpin of the peace process that resulted in the Oslo Accords between Israel and the PLO.

Attention to Conflict

In an ideal world, disputes between actors would never reach beyond the first phase described in Chapter 1: pre-violence. Mediators would be deployed before the parties had a chance to use military force against one another, and escalation to war would be avoided. Even if the dispute were not fully resolved, if violence were prevented, the various costs of war would be avoided. Unfortunately, one of the problems with mediation efforts, and conflict management attempts in general, is that they tend to be initiated relatively late in the game, after a major incident. As we noted in Chapter 4, high-intensity conflicts tend to be correlated with mediation attempts, thus reinforcing the concern that conflicts need to reach a boiling point before they are placed on the international agenda.

Might earlier intervention in conflicts be desirable? If conflicts could be resolved in the first phase of conflict, this is clearly superior to resolution under similar terms later on when the costs of armed confrontation have been paid. Yet this presumes that there is an adequate early warning mechanism for detecting conflicts that have the strong potential for escalation, and therefore merit immediate mediation efforts. Although the international community has advanced systems for early warning to detect tsunamis and humanitarian emergencies, for political and technical reasons the ability to forecast conflict is not as developed or institutionalized. Nevertheless, many disputes are well known because of their history or the presence of claims (e.g. competing claims over territory, demands for autonomy or secession), and thus there is a large set of latent conflicts that would be suitable for mediation.

Disputing parties also must be amenable to mediation in the early phase of conflict. Rational choice theorists predict that disputants would be less inclined to accept mediation then, and less inclined to agree to settlement even if mediation were accepted. Without the necessary information about future settlement terms that armed conflict provides, parties would not a priori agree to an outcome that might be less than future bargaining and fighting might bring. Similarly, proponents of the mutually hurting stalemate model expect that enemies would not come to the table without first experiencing some costs. As desirable as early resolution of conflict might be, there are challenges for mediators to induce parties to come together and ultimately bargain in good faith prior to some crisis or violent episode. Although third parties might seek to encourage disputants to see themselves in a mutually hurting stalemate early in a conflict by urging them to foresee the costs of fighting to come in the future, without tangible evidence of these future costs, such efforts can face stiff resistance from the combatants.

A symmetrical problem for mediation occurs at the other end of the conflict phase spectrum when third parties leave the scene too quickly, even after they have managed to facilitate some kind of agreement. This leaves the disputants to hammer out any differences in the implementation of agreements as well as deal with additional issues that arise. Notably, this deficiency was identified as something associated with less durable agreements. This problem can partly be solved by establishing credible commitments by the third parties to assist the disputants in implementing settlements. As noted above, this can be critical in getting the parties to sign the agreement in the first place as well as enhance its durability. Yet there often remains the need for additional mechanisms for mediation in the aftermath of successful negotiations, especially if the agreement is for a limited cease-fire or represents only a partial settlement. Thus, the challenge for mediators is not to leave too early, along with avoiding the aforementioned problem of arriving too late.

Coordination and Consistency across Conflict Management Techniques

Conflict management approaches, although conceptually distinct, do not occur in isolation with one another. A given conflict might experience a variety of different attempts to deal with it, including verbal appeals for a cease-fires, peace operations, and adjudicatory proceedings as well as mediation. These can occur simultaneously or sequentially. As is evident from the discussion of peacekeeping and mediation in Chapter 5, these approaches are not always compatible and indeed might undermine one another.

One of the challenges for mediation providers is to ensure some coordination and consistency across conflict management efforts. This is complicated in that the actors attempting other conflict management strategies are often quite different from those who are providing mediation. Even multiple mediation attempts by different actors are not well integrated. There is not extensive research or knowledge about the interconnections of conflict management approaches (Owsiak, 2011 is perhaps the first attempt to understand the patterns of interconnections), but there are some possible interactive effects among different approaches. We have seen that peacekeeping might actually harm attempts to get disputants to the bargaining table as well to secure a settlement once they get there (Greig and Diehl, 2005). Yet, at the same time, successful mediation in the form of securing a temporary cease-fire is often a necessary step to achieve the conditions for the initial deployment of a traditional peacekeeping operation; such operations can have great value in saving lives, both through limiting conflict and by facilitating the delivery of humanitarian aid.

There is reason to expect that other conflict management strategies have interactive effects with mediation as well. If adjudication and arbitration efforts are occurring and will provide a future settlement, mediation might undermine those legal mechanisms. In domestic courts, mediation and negotiation that occur simultaneously with legal proceedings, but outside of legal forums, allow participants to "settle out of court" and drop suits and claims against one another. This occurrence is much rarer in international disputes. Were mediation efforts to facilitate a settlement and preempt a legal ruling, they would provide for an immediate outcome, but not necessarily one that is stable in the long run. There is no guarantee that this outcome is optimal, even if accepted by both sides, and the agreement might lack the legitimacy and potential enforceability of a judicial ruling. For example, a decision rendered by the European Court of Justice will have the authority, both normative and administrative, of the European Union behind it whereas a mediated settlement might lack this additional pressure to comply with any commitments made. A failed mediation attempt might be damaging to any judicial outcome. If the losing party in an arbitration hearing finds that its share of the dispute pie is less than what was offered in negotiations, it might seek to reject the decision and reopen the bargaining and/or use military force to prompt a better deal. Verbal strategies at conflict management might assist mediated negotiations if they constitute pressure on all sides to settle. To the extent, however, that they signal support for the position of one side or the other, they might harden bargaining positions and make a final settlement more difficult.

At minimum, mediators need to be cognizant of other conflict management efforts and adapt their behaviors accordingly. Ideally, we would have a strong research base that gave us the necessary information about the pernicious and advantageous ways in which conflict management approaches affect one other, and actors would coordinate their efforts so that the likelihood of success was maximized.

Coercive vs. Collaborative Consistency

In the previous section, we discussed the challenges imposed by the combination of mediation with other conflict management techniques. Those approaches were largely collaborative in that they relied on the cooperation of the parties involved or at least did not attempt to coerce the parties into settling their conflict; at most verbal strategies are designed to persuade rather than compel changes in behavior to produce desirable outcomes. Yet we know that mediation is also often paired with more coercive intervention strategies, specifically those involving military interventions and economic sanctions. Mediation efforts might also operate in the shadow of international actions that further other goals such as holding individuals responsible for war crimes. These more coercive actions pose special challenges for mediators.

Economic sanctions and military interventions can have several purposes. The former are partly normative, designed to show displeasure with one or more sides in a conflict. Military intervention by the international community or individual states might be calculated to favor one side or the other in the conflict in order to help that side win, but the intervention might also be purely humanitarian, designed to ensure the delivery of aid to threatened populations. Yet both military interventions and economic sanctions are intended to impose costs on one or more conflict parties. To the extent that these facilitate mutually hurting stalemates, such actions might complement mediation efforts. Economic sanctions against Serbia and the collaboration of Bosniak and Croat forces during the Bosnian civil war are credited with bringing the Serbs to the bargaining table and signing the Dayton Accords. In the absence of that pressure, Bosnian Serbs might have merely consolidated and extended their gains as they continued the war rather than agreeing to a mediated settlement. Coercive measures that tip the fighting in favor of one side, however, might encourage that actor to continue fighting rather than settle. Furthermore, coercive measures and mediation carried out by the same actor (e.g. the United Nations) might complicate the success of the latter. A disputant might not regard a representative of an organization as an honest broker if that organization is simultaneously punishing or taking military action against it.

The international community has several goals during an ongoing conflict in addition to stopping the fighting and securing a settlement, the primary targets for mediation attempts. Recently, holding those responsible for acts of genocide and other war crimes has become a higher priority. Yet this can pose additional roadblocks to mediators seeking a halt to the fighting and a political settlement to an ongoing war. A political leader (whether governmental or group) that is accused of war crimes or indicted by the International Criminal Court (ICC) has less incentive to give up power if it means that s/he will be subject to prosecution. Thus, dropping an indictment or granting immunity for past crimes might be a condition for making concessions or relinquishing power. Mediation efforts to end the violence in Darfur have been made more complex by the ICC's indictment of Sudanese President Al-Bashir. Similarly, the African Union had called upon its members to ignore the ICC indictment of Libyan leader Gaddafi as it would have complicated the organization's ability to get a negotiated settlement between rebels and the Libyan government. Criminal liability for war crimes could become another disputed issue to be negotiated. If mediators and other parties refuse such negotiations, the mediation effort might collapse. If ICC and other criminal indictments are put on the negotiating table, then this undermines efforts to prosecute war criminals. It would also signal to leaders in the future that they might act with impunity and expect to negotiate their way out of any criminal responsibility later as needed. In trying to balance these goals, mediators will be challenged because the mediation and ICC indictment process run on parallel tracks with neither having direct influence over the other.

Linkages across Three Stages
In Chapter 1, we noted that there are roughly three stages to the conflict management process: getting to the table, securing an agreement, and implementing that agreement. The subsequent analysis summarized the various conditions that are associated with success in those stages, recognizing that those factors are not uniform over the process. It was also evident that the success at one stage did not guarantee success or even progress at subsequent stages. As in the case of Angola, it is possible to get warring sides to negotiate and come to a peace settlement, but problems in implementation can lead to a reversion back to armed conflict and the need to get the disputants back to the table.

One challenge for mediators is to look ahead to the next stages and understand how actions in the present stage might impact success later on. If a mediator is attempting to bring the two sides to the negotiating table, there might be circumstances in which such efforts should be abandoned or not even attempted. Trying to get actors to negotiate could prove futile if the conditions, such as a hurting stalemate, are not present. Yet if those initial conditions occur and enemies agree to mediation, devious objectives or the lack of other ripe or readiness conditions could doom such negotiations to failure. As we identified, failed mediation efforts can have some positive effects. Yet mediators might consider not even attempting mediation if a settlement is unlikely and there is little new groundwork that needs to be laid for future mediation attempts. In part, this was the motivation of US President George W. Bush's administration when it decided not to give much priority to Mideast peace negotiations early in its first term: the failure of the predecessor Clinton administration initiatives and no changes in the environment indicated that renewing mediation at that time would be pointless.

Mediators in the second stage of mediation must recognize that securing an agreement and ensuring a fully implemented peace settlement are interconnected processes. A preliminary agreement, such as a cease-fire, certainly has some benefits, not the least of which is stopping bloodshed and perhaps allowing the delivery of humanitarian assistance. Yet this might also stall progress toward a more expansive settlement. Having the cease-fire backed by a peacekeeping force could lessen the likelihood of future negotiations and their success should they occur – the net effect would be to freeze the status quo, but not necessarily resolve the conflict. Thus, mediators might sometimes choose to resist limited agreements in the short term in favor of pursuing comprehensive settlements even as the latter are often elusive.

The willingness of actors to commit to a peace agreement is partly influenced by their expectations about how effectively and honestly the agreement will be implemented. Thus, mediators would be wise to introduce incentives for compliance and third-party guarantees on implementation during the second stage. These might not change the actual terms of agreement on the disputed issues involved, but they can make the rivals more likely to sign the agreement and ensure that it is successfully implemented thereafter, thus producing not simply an agreement but a durable one.

A myopic focus on short-term achievements might produce some successes, but the payoffs are bigger and better in the long run when mediators recognize the interconnections between conflict management stages and adapt their strategies accordingly.

Win-Win Solutions

Traditional conceptions envisage a mediator facilitating a process in which disputing parties each make concessions and agree to a settlement that involves something less than the preferred position of each of them. Analogies such as dividing a pie or meeting in the middle reinforce this view. Yet we know that some settlements are better than others, and merely getting to an agreement is no guarantee of long-term stability. Ideally, a settlement will be regarded as "fair" by all sides and provide a net benefit to all the participants. This is likely to undermine future spoiling attempts as well as mitigate incentives for the signatories to reopen negotiations or renew conflicts. Colloquially, the best of these solutions are known as "win-win" outcomes. At the most extreme are solutions that are "super-optimum" (Nagel, 1997), which allow all sides to come out ahead of their best initial expectations, and to do so simultaneously. Thus, a further challenge for mediators is to move beyond securing an agreement to one that has win-win properties.

Constructing win-win solutions, or indeed any mutually agreeable solutions, might be impossible for some conflicts. In other instances, the methods for achieving better solutions will be context-specific. It might take expanding the issues in negotiations in order to permit better trade-offs and maximize values on the salient issues for each side. Mediators might also offer carrots (e.g. financial aid or security guarantees) to increase the payoffs of the disputants, and make the final agreement superior to what the parties might have achieved alone or by just dividing benefits among extant issues.

Brams and Taylor (1999) offer several criteria for assessing the fairness of an agreement and whether it can be considered the best possible; three key points stand out. First is the "proportionality" of the agreement, in that each side should perceive that it got at least half of what it wanted. Note that disputes are not necessarily zero-sum, and one enemy can place a higher value on one disputed issue as compared to another issue valued by its rival. Second, the terms of the agreement should be "envy-free" in that no party should be willing to give up what it has in the agreement for something that the opponent has. That is, each party should recognize that it can't do much better than what it agreed to, a condition likely to augur well for stability in the long run. Third, the agreement should be "efficient," in that all benefits have been allocated and there is nothing left over to negotiate. Perhaps no agreement can be perfect in every dimension, but mediators can strive to maximize the gains made in an agreement, and thereby enhance its likely durability and obviate the need for further negotiations.

Intractable Conflicts

Being successful at mediation is always a challenge, but the problem is acute when dealing with the most difficult conflicts. Mediation analysts (Crocker et al., 2004; 2005a; Bercovitch, 2005) have classified such situations as "intractable conflicts." Others have used the term "enduring rivalries," whether in describing interstate (Diehl and Goertz, 2000) or intrastate competitions (DeRouen and Bercovitch, 2008). Regardless of the moniker, these conflicts share a number of characteristics. They tend to be protracted, often lasting decades rather than months or a few years. They also experience frequent and repeated episodes of violent conflict. Over time, enemy images, security policy orientations, and public opinion reinforce the hostility between the actors. The issues and the parties' bargaining positions also usually make it difficult to construct settlements that are acceptable to all. Typical examples of such conflicts include those between India and Pakistan, Israel and the Palestinians, and various conflicts in Bosnia and Sudan.

Intractable conflicts are the most difficult to solve, but because of their repeated militarized confrontations and their severity, they also tend to attract the most mediation attempts. Not surprisingly though, they have a high failure rate. Crocker et al. (2004) point to, but don't endorse, several alternatives for mediators that largely involve ignoring these conflicts and concentrating on those that are more amenable to management. Having the international community completely ignore enduring rivalries and intractable conflicts is a morally questionable and strategically foolish option. These are the conflicts that are the most likely to escalate to war and have spillover effects on neighbors. Furthermore, such conflicts consume enormous resources and diplomatic attention that might be directed to other global and societal problems. Ignoring them brings many costs. Doing so ensures that there is no mediation failure, but no success at resolving differences either.

Other alternatives to concerted mediation, such as deferring conflict management actions to others, might be rational for individual actors but are likely to produce the same outcome as ignoring the conflict. Actors will free ride on providing the public good of mediation, especially when the prospects for success are limited; the net effect is that most or all actors will pass the buck and no actor will ultimately intervene. Undertaking mediation only when there is fighting or high costs are unavoidable because of the risks of escalation or negative externalities is also not a compelling strategy. These moments might not be optimal for achieving a settlement and mediators are likely to concentrate on short-term concerns such as cease-fires rather than broader settlement concerns.

Mediators cannot afford to sit out the most difficult circumstances, but there are some strategies that might be applied with respect to intractable conflicts. A number of suggestions (see e.g. Crocker et al., 2004) are merely good mediation practice in general, including counteracting destructive negotiating behavior by the parties and seeking to minimize the impact of spoilers. Nevertheless, some concerns are especially salient in intractable conflicts and are reflective of the limits that mediators face (Crocker et al. 2005b). First, mediators need to be attuned to issues of timing and specifically shifts to more favorable environments for negotiation. These windows of opportunity might be rarer in intractable conflicts, and mediators need to recognize them and jump through. Coordination between different mediation and conflict management efforts is also more critical in this context, lest opportunities be missed or undermined. Indeed, Crocker et al. (2005b) note that ineffective mediation can be especially damaging in the context of intractable conflict, citing weak US efforts in Sudan during the 1990s as indicative of when such diplomacy might have made things worse. Finally, it might be that given irreconcilable differences, mediators sometimes might have to be content to freeze the status quo, albeit without violence, rather than aim to resolve a conflict fully.

Future Research Agendas

Our understanding of international mediation has been greatly broadened and deepened in the last two decades. Previously, most analyses were single-case reflections by insider participants. Many of these contained valuable insights, but lacked the identification of broader patterns and relationships that allowed generalizations applicable to other cases and valid prescriptions to guide future policy making. Despite the expansion of mediation studies and their improvement in theoretical and methodological sophistication, there remain a number of issues and questions that should form the basis for future inquiry, thereby hopefully adding to our knowledge base.

Multiple and Multiparty Mediation Attempts
In Chapter 2, we noted that some conflicts receive multiple mediation attempts, sometimes by the same actor, but often by new actors as well. There is some evidence that successive mediation attempts serve a positive function and that success is enhanced in the long run. In contrast, some conflicts receive only a single mediation attempt and others attract no third-party diplomacy at all. Yet we know very little about why repeated mediations occur (Beardsley, 2010). It is not merely the case that successful mediations end the process as success comes in varying degrees, often leaving unresolved issues; even full settlements prompt further mediation to assure effective implementation. It is also not the case that failure automatically breeds more diplomatic efforts even though failure might be more likely than success to generate further mediation. Mediators and the international community sometimes give up and do not attempt to manage certain conflicts. It is likely that the history of conflict management in the dispute has an impact on multiple mediations (Melin, 2011), but that is probably not the only important element. Because of the resources expended and the ultimate effect on success, we need to know more about multiple mediation attempts.

Some segments of the scholarly literature suggest that multiparty mediation can be beneficial because it can bring both more resources and more third parties capable of devising a settlement to the conflict. Multiparty mediation, by bringing more actors into the process, also raises the risk of miscommunication, buck-passing, and forum shopping. Understanding when multiparty mediation is most likely to be beneficial and when it would be least useful would be an important addition to our knowledge about mediation.

Failed Efforts

In a related fashion, we know less than we should about the impact of failed mediations, the most common outcome. Most research has emphasized the positive aspects of even failed mediation, such as clarifying issues and establishing the parameters of an agreement. Yet there are some likely deleterious effects as well. If disputants learn from their interactions with one another, it makes sense to expect that at least some failed efforts at diplomacy will have negative consequences for the future relationship between the parties. Failed diplomacy may serve to "teach" some disputants that they cannot resolve their dispute through dialogue and force them to rely upon more coercive means to settle their dispute. Previous studies suggest that as mediation fails, states should intensify violence as a means of imposing costs on the other side and forcing capitulation; we do not know whether this is the case empirically or not. Furthermore, indecisive outcomes in conflict and failed mediation efforts might serve to create or prolong enduring rivalries (Shin and Diehl, 2008), and indeed one element for the maintenance of such rivalries is the failure of conflict management (Goertz et. al. 2005).

Selection Effects

Selection effects refer to the process in which cases are chosen for analysis and how this influences the kinds of conclusions that we draw. Selection effects have at least two notable implications for our analyses of mediation. There is a tendency for analysts to focus only on conflicts that cross a certain threshold of severity; often some level of violence has to occur or is very likely. Ignored are lesser conflicts that might also be mediated or at least amenable to mediation. Thus, the conclusions that we draw about the conditions for success really only apply to the more severe conflicts. In some sense, this is acceptable because it is these conflicts that are the most dangerous and have worst consequences for the international community. Yet it also means that we ignore the possibility of mediation intervention in the first phase of conflict, before any violence has occurred and when success might bring a number of benefits. Future study might consider mediation at lower conflict thresholds and how it might differ (if at all) in terms of when and how mediation is effective.

From a methodological standpoint, studies too often look only at cases of mediation and ignore those conflicts in which mediation did not occur (Bercovitch and Gartner, 2006). The analysis then is a cross-sectional one on a biased sample. Yet we know that the process of choosing mediation might be related to the conditions that lead to its success, something that cannot be determined if we only consider cases in which mediators are able to get disputants to the table. Past research has shown that the factors affecting mediation onset are different from those that influence getting an agreement, but this does not mean that the first-stage processes do not affect what happens when actors try to reach a settlement.

Costs

The costs of conflict are a central component of the mutually hurting stalemate idea and a series of other formulations on the conditions that bring states to the table and get them to come to an agreement. Yet in most analyses, there is little discussion of exactly what these costs are and which ones are most salient (Shin and Diehl, 2008). It is not clear whether such costs are accumulated, current, or prospective. Zartman (2007b) asserts that the salient ones are "optimally" those associated with impending or recently avoided catastrophes. Impending catastrophes imply prospective costs, whereas the idea that recently avoided disasters bring states to the bargaining table makes little sense: if large costs were successfully avoided and not likely to occur again in the short term, why should actors seek negotiation based on the logic of cost-benefit calculations? The specification of accumulated costs suggests a convergence with timing, as it usually takes an extended period for losses to register, although especially intense fighting may precipitate this sooner rather than later.

Current costs should be most salient to political leaders. Nevertheless, such costs tend to vary significantly over time, suggesting that they may be unreliable and fleeting elements of the pain necessary for mutually hurting stalemate. Future costs would likely have the greatest influence on the willingness of actors to negotiate, provided that the shadow of the future was not too long. Yet these are notoriously difficult to judge, particularly in empirical terms.

Beyond the temporal aspects of costs, there is little specification in recent work about the kinds of pain necessary to precipitate mutually hurting stalemate. Fighting in war usually brings to mind human losses in terms of casualties. Yet there may also be the financial and political expenditures associated with continued rivalry and war, especially if accumulated costs are the relevant benchmark. Are these two types of costs equivalent or substitutable? Might there be different cost sensitivities, in terms of source, among the actors involved? Some next steps in research would be to consider which kinds of costs are most critical in affecting the mediation propensity of enemies, and simultaneously consider whether such losses are ones borne in the past, present, or prospectively.

New Areas of Concern

Previous items on the research agenda have been generally those that represent extensions on earlier work or seek to address gaps or questions suggested by that work. Yet in the adolescent stage of mediation research, there are a whole series of questions that have been unexplored or even not asked at all. We outline several of the most interesting and fruitful ones below.

Most mediation studies employ narrow, cross-sectional analysis in which atomized cases are compared with one another and assumed to be largely independent of one another. At best, past mediation attempts in the same conflict are sometimes included as an explanatory variable. Yet analysts might consider variation *within* individual cases, specifically how preferences change during a conflict or mediation attempt (Beardsley, 2010); this would allow us to track the kinds of processes that occur when mutually hurting stalemates arise and mediators change perceptions. It would also be useful to explore how the effects of mediation in one conflict diffuse to other conflicts. Various conflicts are sometimes interconnected (e.g. Israel's disputes with Lebanon, Iran, and Hamas) and if nothing else actors in conflicts are attentive to the processes and settlement terms of other mediated outcomes, even if they do not have a direct stake. Thus, mediation studies, which already have looked at the time dependence of mediation cases, should also consider how such cases are connected across geographic space and social networks.

Scholars have used a variety of variables to account for mediation outcomes, and we in Chapter 4 sorted these into a number of categories including those related to the mediator, the conflict context, and the disputants. Yet two sets of factors that have become increasingly prominent in studies of interstate and intrastate conflict have not yet found their way into mediation studies. Rather than merely focus on costs, greater attention might be paid to the economic resources possessed by the key players, both conflicting and third parties (Bercovitch and Gartner, 2009). Abundant (or scarce) resources will affect the cost calculations of the rivals as well as suggest what kinds of mediators might best be able to alter payoff schemes by increasing the size of the pie or imposing additional costs on the rivals. In addition, the impact of domestic political factors and public opinion is largely ignored in mediation studies (Melin, 2011). Nevertheless, an actor's willingness to come to the table, sign an agreement, and faithfully implement it will be influenced by her domestic political constituency and the (dis)incentives therein that influence the future political prospects of leaders who take those actions. At the same time, third parties seeking to manage a conflict can also influence the domestic politics of the disputants, potentially providing another source of leverage for mediators to make parties get to the table and reach a settlement. There are many extant approaches available, but incorporating domestic politics into explanations of mediation behavior is overdue.

Appendix: Mediated Conflicts, 1945–1999

	Start Year of First Mediation	Start Year of Last Mediation	Total Mediation on Efforts
The Chinese Civil War	1945	1947	5
The Greek Civil War	1945	1950	16
The USSR–Iran: Azerbaijan Crisis	1945	1954	4
The Netherlands–The Dutch East Indies: Indonesian Independence	1946	1946	1
France–Indochina: Independence Struggle	1947	1947	1
Albania–United Kingdom: The Corfu Channel Dispute	1948	1948	1
Dominican Republic–Haiti/Cuba: Regional Aggression	1948	1948	1
Pakistan–India: The First Kashmir War	1948	1948	2
The Costa Rican Civil War	1948	1948	2
The Israeli War of Independence	1948	1949	3
The USSR–The Western Allies: The Berlin Airlift Crisis	1948	1949	12
The Malayan Emergency	1948	1964	27
India–Hyderabad: Secession Attempt	1949	1949	2
Burma: The Kuomintang Conflict	1949	1951	5
Nicaragua–Costa Rica: Border Conflict	1949	1998	17
Burma: Civil War and Insurgency	1950	1950	2
Syria–Lebanon: The Syrian Exiles Dispute	1950	1956	3
Eritrea–Ethiopia: Independence Attempt	1950	1956	4
Afghanistan–Pakistan: Border/Pathan Conflict	1951	1951	5
Afghanistan–Pakistan: The Pathan Conflict	1951	1994	7
The Korean War	1952	1960	5
Syria–Israel: The Lake Tiberias/Huleh Dispute	1953	1953	1

	Start Year of First Mediation	Start Year of Last Mediation	Total Mediation on Efforts
Egypt–The UK: The Suez Canal Zone Dispute	1953	1954	6
Yugoslavia–Italy: The Trieste Dispute	1953	1956	3
Argentina–Chile: The Beagle Channel Dispute	1954	1955	2
Saudi Arabia–Oman/UK: The Buraimi Crisis	1954	1996	38
Israel–Jordan: The West Bank Border Conflict	1955	1955	1
Cambodia–Siam (Thailand): Temple of Preah Vihear and Border Conflict	1955	1959	4
China–The USA/Taiwan: The Quemoy Confrontation	1956	1956	1
The Guatemalan Civil War and Insurgency	1956	1956	1
Algerian Independence	1956	1956	1
Nicaragua–Costa Rica: Invasion Attempt	1956	1957	2
Cyprus–The United Kingdom: The Enosis Movement	1956	1959	5
Syria–Israel: The Lake Tiberias Dispute	1956	1961	2
The Dominican Republic–Cuba/ Venezuela: Dominican Tyranny and The Exiles Conflict	1957	1957	1
Israel–Jordan: The Mt. Scopus Conflict	1957	1957	1
The Suez War	1957	1957	1
The USSR–Hungary: The Hungarian Uprising of 1956	1958	1958	1
Nicaragua–Honduras: The Mocoran Seizure	1958	1958	1
Israel–Syria: The Golan Heights Conflict	1958	1958	1
Morocco–Spain: The Sahara Conflict	1958	1958	3
The Panama Revolutionaries Conflict	1958	1989	35
Egypt–Sudan: Border Dispute	1959	1959	1
France–Tunisia: The Military Bases Conflict	1959	1959	1
The First Lebanese Civil War	1959	1959	1
The First Laotian Civil War	1959	1966	3
Syria–Iraq: The Mosul Revolt	1960	1960	1
Cuba–Haiti: The Haitan Exiles Conflict	1960	1960	1
The Congo Conflict	1960	1960	2

	Start Year of First Mediation	Start Year of Last Mediation	Total Mediation on Efforts
Afghanistan–Pakistan: The Pathan Conflict	1960	1962	11
The USA–Cuba: The Bay of Pigs	1961	1961	1
Iraq–Kuwait: The Kuwaiti Independence Crisis	1961	1961	2
India–Portugal: The Goa Conflict	1961	1963	4
Indonesia–Malaysia: The Borneo Conflict	1962	1962	1
Indonesia–The Netherlands: The West Irian (Irian Jaya) Administration Dispute	1962	1962	1
Venezuela–Guyana [UK]: The Essequibo River Dispute	1962	1962	2
Chile–Bolivia: The Lauca River Dam Dispute	1962	1964	4
Syria–Israel: The Lake Tiberias Dispute	1963	1963	1
The USA–The USSR: The Cuban Missile Crisis	1963	1963	1
North Yemen: The Royalist Rebellion	1963	1963	4
India–China: Border War	1963	1965	3
Somalia–Kenya/ Ethiopia: Somali Expansionism	1963	1966	8
China–USSR: The Ussuri River Conflict	1963	1967	3
Haiti–Dominican Republic (USA): Exiles Asylum and Invasion Attempt	1963	1967	6
The First Sudan Civil War	1963	1967	13
Algeria–Morocco: The Tindouf War	1963	1972	16
Cuba–Venezuela: Terrorism and Invasion Attempt	1963	1985	4
The Cypriot Civil War	1964	1964	1
Niger–Dahomey (Benin): The Lete Island Dispute	1964	1964	1
Somalia–Ethiopia: The First Ogaden War	1964	1964	3
Panama –The USA: The Flag Riots	1964	1964	8
Rwanda–Burundi: The Hutu–Tutsi Ethnic Conflict	1964	1968	25
South Vietnam–Cambodia: Border Conflict	1965	1965	1
Ghana–Upper Volta: Ghanaian Border Dispute	1965	1965	2
Syria–Israel: Border Incidents	1965	1965	8
North Vietnam–The USA: The Vietnam War	1965	1966	3

	Start Year of First Mediation	Start Year of Last Mediation	Total Mediation on Efforts
Israel–Jordan: Border Incidents	1965	1966	4
Eritrea–Ethiopia: War of Secession	1965	1966	8
Colombian Guerrilla Insurgency	1965	1969	3
India–Pakistan: Border Skirmishes	1966	1966	1
The USA–The Dominican Republic: The Constitutionalist Rebellion	1966	1966	1
India–Pakistan: The Second Kashmir War	1967	1967	5
Chad–Sudan: The First Chad Civil War	1967	1968	4
Namibian Independence Struggle	1967	1969	15
Ghana–Guinea: Nkrumah Tensions	1967	1971	21
Bolivia: Attempted Revolution	1968	1970	2
Rhodesia: Zimbabwean Independence Struggle	1969	1970	7
Guinea–Ivory Coast: Hostage Crisis	1970	1971	3
Israel–The Arab States: The Six Day War	1970	1971	11
Nigeria–Biafra: Secession Attempt	1971	1972	2
Congo (Zaire)–Rwanda: The Mercenaries Dispute	1971	1973	7
El Salvador–Honduras: The Football War	1972	1972	2
Mindanao–The Philippines: Muslim Secession Insurgency	1972	1972	4
The PLO–Jordan: Coup Attempt	1972	1986	9
Guinean–Portugal: The Conakry Raids	1973	1975	2
Uganda–Tanzania: Border Clashes	1973	1976	3
North Yemen–South Yemen: Border Conflict	1973	1979	26
Iceland–United Kingdom (West Germany and Denmark): The Cod War	1973	1997	21
Oman–South Yemen: The Dhofar Rebellion	1974	1974	1
Iran–Iraq: Border War	1974	1975	2
Equatorial Guinea–Gabon: The Corisco Bay Islands Dispute	1974	1975	4
Ethiopia–Somalia: The Second Ogaden War	1974	1976	2
Iraq–Kuwait: Border Incidents	1974	1976	6
Israel–Egypt: The Yom Kippur War	1974	1979	25
Israel–Syria: The Yom Kippur War	1974	1984	11
The Cyprus Conflict: Invasion and Partition	1974	1995	66

	Start Year of First Mediation	Start Year of Last Mediation	Total Mediation on Efforts
Israel–Lebanon: Arab Infiltrators	1975	1975	3
Morocco–Mauritania: The Western Saharan Conflict	1975	1990	80
Mali–Upper Volta (Burkina Faso): Border Conflict	1975	1998	56
Angola–South Africa: Intervention and Civil War	1975	1999	99
The Second Lebanese Civil War	1976	1976	2
Syria–Iraq: The Euphrates Dispute	1976	1976	3
East Timor–Indonesia: Independence Struggle	1976	1999	25
Zaire–Angola: Border War	1977	1977	1
Mozambique–South Africa: Intervention and Civil War	1977	1977	1
Uganda–Kenya: Border Incidents	1977	1977	6
The Kurds–Iraq: Kurdish Autonomy	1978	1978	2
Chad–Libya: The Aozou Strip Dispute	1978	1978	2
El Salvador–Honduras: Border Incidents	1978	1979	2
El Salvador: The Salvadorian Civil War	1978	1979	7
Zaire–Angola: The First Invasion of Shaba	1978	1980	11
Egypt–Libya: Border War	1978	1993	8
Nicaragua–Costa Rica: Border Incidents	1979	1979	2
The Second Chad Civil War	1979	1979	2
Israel–Lebanon/PLO: Border Conflict	1979	1980	11
Nicaragua–Costa Rica: Border Incidents	1979	1987	9
Tanzania–Uganda: Ouster of the Amin Regime	1980	1980	1
The USSR–Afghanistan: Intervention and Civil War	1980	1991	33
Cambodia (Kampuchea)–Vietnam: The Cambodian Civil War	1980	1998	43
North Yemen–South Yemen: Border War	1981	1981	1
Morocco–Algeria: Western Sahara Nationalism	1981	1981	4
Israel–Syria: Air Incidents	1981	1994	41
Iran–The USA: The Hostage Crisis	1981	1999	79
Cambodia (Kampuchea)–Thailand: Border Conflict	1982	1985	18
Honduras–Nicaragua: The Contra War	1982	1986	11

	Start Year of First Mediation	Start Year of Last Mediation	Total Mediation Efforts
The Iran–Iraq War	1983	1994	14
Ecuador–Peru: Border War	1983	1999	20
Cameroon–Nigeria: Border Incident	1983	1999	22
The Ugandan Civil War	1984	1994	38
Israel–Lebanon: The Israeli Military Invasion of Lebanon	1984	1999	65
The United Kingdom–Argentina: The Falklands War	1985	1985	1
Libya–Chad: Intervention and Third Chad Civil War	1985	1986	4
Sri Lanka: The Tamil Conflict	1986	1986	2
The Second Sudan Civil War	1986	1986	2
Israel–Lebanon: The Security Zone	1986	1987	2
Turkey–Greece: Naval Incidents	1987	1987	1
The Kurds–Turkey: Secession Struggle	1989	1989	3
Nicaragua–Costa Rica: Border Incidents	1989	1992	8
Mali–Burkina Faso: Border War	1989	1999	16
India–Pakistan: The Siachin Glacier and Kashmir Conflicts	1990	1991	19
Qatar–Bahrain: The Hawar Islands Dispute	1990	1994	9
Surinam Guerrilla Insurgency	1990	1998	66
Togo–Ghana: Overthrow Attempt	1990	1999	57
The Somalia Civil War	1991	1994	3
Burundi: The Hutu Conflict	1991	1998	62
Bouganville–Papua New Guinea: Secession Attempt	1991	1998	66
Georgia–South Ossetia: Abkhazia Secession War	1991	1998	274
Mauritania–Senegal: Border Incidents	1991	1999	13
Yugoslavian Civil War: The Balkans War	1991	1999	14
The Liberian Civil War	1991	1999	95
Tuareg–Niger: Confrontation and Reprisals	1992	1992	1
Senegal: The Casamamnce Rebellion	1992	1992	1
Tuareg–Mali: The Tuareg Conflict	1992	1992	7
Iraq–Kuwait/The Coalition Forces: The Gulf War	1992	1997	39

	Start Year of First Mediation	Start Year of Last Mediation	Total Mediation on Efforts
Azerbaijan–Armenia: Nagorno-Karabakh Conflict	1993	1993	1
Rwandan Invasion	1993	1994	34
Gagauz/ Dnestr–Moldova: Secession Attempt	1993	1995	10
Liberia–Sierra Leone: Intervention and the Sierra Leone Civil War	1993	1999	4
The Djibouti Civil War	1993	1999	8
Iran–UAE, Egypt : Abu Musa and Tunb Islands Dispute	1993	1999	19
The Tajikistan Conflict	1994	1994	1
Saudi Arabia–Qatar: Border Incidents	1994	1994	1
Russia–Chechnya: The Caucuses Conflict (Ingush–Northern Ossetia)	1994	1994	3
Egypt–Sudan: The Halaib Dispute	1994	1994	6
The Yemen Civil War	1994	1995	2
Nigeria–Cameroon: The Diamond and Djabane Islands Dispute	1994	1999	9
Ghana–Togo: Border Incidents	1994	1999	49
The USA–Haiti: Aristide's Return From Exile	1995	1995	8
Iraq–The Coalition: Kuwaiti Border Tensions	1995	1997	11
Saudi Arabia–Yemen: Border Clash	1995	1999	73
Ecuador–Peru: Cenepa Confrontation	1996	1996	1
Comoros: Coup Attempt	1996	1998	10
Eritrea–Yemen: The Invasion of the Hunish Islands	1996	1998	11
Cyprus–Turkey: Incidents along Cyprus–Northern Cyprus border	1996	1999	10
Uganda: Civil Conflict	1996	1999	15
Ecuador–Peru: Territorial Dispute	1996	1999	18
China–Taiwan: Third Taiwan Strait Crisis	1996	1999	27
Niger: Military Coup	1997	1997	1
Democratic Republic of the Congo–Congo Wars (First & Second)	1997	1999	23
North Korea–South Korea: Incidents	1997	1999	27
The Republic of the Congo Civil War	1997	1999	72
Djibouti: Civil Conflict	1998	1998	1

	Start Year of First Mediation	Start Year of Last Mediation	Total Mediation on Efforts
Lesotho: Anti-Government Mutiny	1998	1998	5
Eritrean–Ethiopian War	1998	1999	10
Kosovo War	1998	1999	11
The Guinea-Bissau Civil War	1999	1999	1
Guinea–Liberia: Border Incidents	1999	1999	2

References and Suggested Readings

Aggestam, K. and C. Jönsson. 1997. "(Un)Ending Conflict: Challenges in Post-War Bargaining." *Millennium: Journal of International Studies* 26(3): 771–794.

Akcinaroglu, S., J. M. DiCicco, and E. Radziszewski. 2011. "Avalanches and Olive Branches: A Multimethod Analysis of Disasters and Peacemaking in Interstate Rivalries." *Political Research Quarterly* 64(2): 260–275.

Allen, S. H. and T. Vincent. 2011. "Bombing to Bargain? The Air War for Kosovo." *Foreign Policy Analysis* 7(1): 1–26.

Allport, G. 1954. *The Nature of Prejudice.* Reading, MA: Addison-Wesley Publishing.

Amir, Y. 1998. "Contact Hypothesis in Ethnic Relations." In *The Handbook of Interethnic Coexistence,* E. Weiner, ed. New York: Continuum.

Andersen, P., J. Bumgardner, J. M. Greig, and P. F. Diehl. 2001. "Turning Down the Heat: Influences on Conflict Management in Enduring Rivalries." *International Interactions* 27(3): 239–274.

Ayres, R. W. 1997. "Mediating International Conflicts: Is Image Change Necessary?" *Journal of Peace Research* 34(4): 431–448.

Bajpai, K. 2003. "Managing Conflict in South Asia." In *Regional Conflict Management,* P. F. Diehl and J. Lepgold, eds. Lanham, MD: Rowman and Littlefield.

Beardsley, K. 2006. *Politics by Means Other than War: Understanding International Mediation.* Dissertation. San Diego, CA: University of California.

Beardsley, K. 2008. "Agreement without Peace? International Mediation and Time Inconsistency Problems." *American Journal of Political Science* 52(4): 723–740.

Beardsley, K. 2009. "Intervention Without Leverage: Explaining the

Prevalence of Weak Mediators." *International Interactions* 35(3): 272–297.

Beardsley, K. 2010. "Pain, Pressure, and Political Cover: Explaining Mediation Incidence." *Journal of the Peace Research* 47(4): 395–406.

Beardsley, K. 2011. *The Mediation Dilemma*. Ithaca, NY: Cornell University Press.

Bellamy, A. 2009. *Responsibility to Protect*. Cambridge: Polity Press.

Bentley, K. and R. Southall. 2005. *An African Peace Process: Mandela, South Africa and Burundi*. Cape Town, South Africa: Human Sciences Research Council. Available at: http://www.hsrcpress.ac.za/product. php [Accessed May 25, 2011].

Bercovitch, J. 1984. *Social Conflicts and Third Parties: Strategies of Conflict Resolution*. Boulder, CO: Westview Press.

Bercovitch, J. 1989. "International Dispute Mediation." In *Mediation Research: The Process and Effectiveness of Third Party Intervention*, K. Kressel and D. Pruitt, eds. San Francisco: Jossey-Bass.

Bercovitch, J. 1997. "Conflict Management and the Oslo Experience: Assessing the Success of Israeli–Palestinian Peacemaking." *International Negotiation* 2(2): 217–235.

Bercovitch, J. 2002. "Introduction: Putting Mediation into Context." In *Studies in International Mediaton*, J. Bercovitch, ed. New York: Palgrave MacMillan.

Bercovitch, J. 2004. International Conflict Management Database. Christchurch, New Zealand. Data and Coding Manual.

Bercovitch, J. 2005. "Mediation in the Most Resistant Cases." In *Grasping the Nettle: Analyzing Cases of Intractable Conflict*, C. A. Crocker, F. O. Hampson, and P. Aall, eds. Washington: United States Institute of Peace Press.

Bercovitch, J. and K. DeRouen. 2005. "Managing Ethnic Civil Wars: Assessing the Determinants of Successful Mediation." *Civil Wars* 7(1): 98–116.

Bercovitch, J. and P. F. Diehl. 1997. "Conflict Management of Enduring Rivalries: Frequency, Timing, and Short-Term Impact of Mediation." *International Interactions* 22(4): 299–320.

Bercovitch, J. and S. Gartner. 2006. "Is There Method in the Madness of Mediation? Some Lessons for Mediators from Quantitative Studies of Mediation." *International Interactions* 32(4): 329–354.

Bercovitch, J. and A. Houston. 1993. "Influence of Mediator Characteristics and Behavior on the Success of Mediation in

International Relations." *International Journal of Conflict Management* 4(4): 297–321.

Bercovitch, J. and A. Houston. 2000. "Why Do they Do it Like this? An Analysis of the Factors Influencing Mediation Behavior in International Conflicts." *Journal of Conflict Resolution* 44(2): 170–202.

Bercovitch, J. and R. Jackson. 2009. *Conflict Resolution in the Twenty First Century: Principles, Methods and Approaches.* Ann Arbor: University of Michigan Press.

Bercovitch, J. and A. Kadayifci-Orellana. 2009. "Religion and Mediation: The Role of Faith-Based Actors in International Conflict Resolution." *International Negotiation* 14(1): 175–204.

Bercovitch, J. and J. Langley. 1993. "The Nature of the Dispute and the Effectiveness of International Mediation." *Journal of Conflict Resolution* 37(4): 670–691.

Bercovitch, J. and P. Regan. 2004. "Mediation and International Conflict Management: A Review and Analysis." In *Multiple Paths to Knowledge in International Relations,* Z. Maoz, A. Mintz, T. C. Morgan, G. Palmer, and R.J. Stoll, eds. Lanham, MD: Lexington Books.

Bercovitch, J. and G. Schneider. 2000. "Who Mediates? The Political Economy of International Conflict Management." *Journal of Peace Research* 37(2): 145–165.

Bercovitch, J., J. T. Anagnoson, and D. L. Wille. 1991. "Some Conceptual Issues and Empirical Trends in the Study of Successful Mediation in International Relations." *Journal of Peace Research* 28(1): 7–17.

Bercovitch, J., P. F. Diehl, and G. Goertz. 1997. "The Management and Termination of Protracted Interstate Conflicts: Conceptual and Empirical Considerations." *Millennium* 26(3): 751–770.

Bien, W. J. 2000. "The Oslo Channel: Benefits of a Neutral Facilitator to Secret Negotiations." In *Words over War: Mediation and Arbitration to Prevent Deadly Conflict,* M. Greenberg, J. Barton, and M. McGuinness, eds. Lanham, MD: Rowman and Littlefield Publishers.

Bohmelt, T. 2010. "Why Many Cooks if they Can Spoil the Broth? The Determinants of Multi-Party Mediation." *papers.ssrn.com:* 1–35. Available at: http://papers.ssrn.com/sol3/papers.cfm?abstract_id= 1644244 [Accessed April 21, 2011].

Boutros-Ghali, B. 1995. *An Agenda for Peace,* 2nd ed. New York: United Nations.

Brahm, E. 2003. "Hurting Stalemate Stage." The Beyond Intractability

Knowledge Base Project. Available at: www.beyondintractability.org/essay/stalemate/. [Accessed July 23, 2011].

Brams, S. and A. Taylor. 1996. *Fair Division: From Cake-Cutting to Dispute Resolution*. Cambridge: Cambridge University Press.

Brams, S. and A. Taylor. 1999. *The Win-Win Solution*. New York: W. W. Norton.

Cederman, L., A. Wimmer, and B. Min. 2010. "Why Do Ethnic Groups Rebel? New Data and Analysis." *World Politics* 62(1): 87–119.

Cetinyan, R. 2002. "Ethnic Bargaining in the Shadow of Third party Intervention." *International Organization* 56 (4): 645–677.

Cha, V. 2003. "The Dilemma of Regional Security in East Asia: Multilateralism versus Bilateralism." In *Regional Conflict Management*, P. F. Diehl and J. Lepgold, eds. Lanham, MD: Rowman and Littlefield.

Colaresi, M., K. Rasler, and W. Thompson. 2008. *Strategic Rivalries in World Politics*. Cambridge: Cambridge University Press.

Collier, P. and A. Hoeffler. 2004. "Greed and Grievance in Civil War." *Oxford Economic Papers* 56(4): 663–695.

Collier, P., A. Hoeffler, and N. Soderbom. 2008. "Post-Conflict Risks." *Journal of Peace Research* 45(4): 461–478.

Cook, S. W. 1971. *The Effect of Unintended Interracial Contact upon Racial Interaction and Attitude Change*. Washington: Department of Health, Education, and Welfare.

Cook, S. W. 1984. "Cooperative Interaction in Multiethnic Contexts." In *Groups in Contact: The Psychology of Desegregation*, N. Miller and M. B. Brewer, eds. Orlando: Academic.

Correlates of War Project. 2008. "State System Membership List, v2008.1." Available at: http://correlatesofwar.org.

Cousens, E. and C. Cater. 2001. *Toward Peace in Bosnia: Implementing the Dayton Accords*. Boulder, CO: Lynne Rienner Publishers.

Crescenzi, M., K. M. Kadera, S. Mitchell, and C. Thyne. 2011. "A Supply Side Theory of Mediation." *International Studies Quarterly* (forthcoming).

Crocker, C. A. 1992. *High Noon in Southern Africa*. New York: Norton.

Crocker, C. A, F. O. Hampson, and P. Aall. 1999. *Herding Cats: Multiparty Mediation in a Complex World*. Washington: United States Institute of Peace Press.

Crocker, C .A., F. O. Hampson, and P. Aall. 2001. "A Crowded Stage: Liabilities and Benefits of Multiparty Mediation." *International Studies Perspectives* 2(1): 51–67.

Crocker, C. A., F. O. Hampson, and P. Aall. 2004. *Taming Intractable Conflicts: Mediation in the Hardest Cases.* Washington: United States Institute of Peace Press.

Crocker, C. A., F. O. Hampson, and P. Aall, eds. 2005a. *Grasping the Nettle: Analyzing Cases of Intractable Conflict.* Washington: United States Institute of Peace Press.

Crocker, C. A., F. O. Hampson, and P. Aall. 2005b. "Conclusion: From Intractable to Tractable – the Outlook and Implications for Third Parties." In Crocker, Hampson, and Aall (2005a).

Curran, D., J. K. Sebenius, and M. Watkins. 2004. "Two Paths to Peace: Contrasting George Mitchell in Northern Ireland with Richard Holbrooke in Bosnia-Herzegovina." *Negotiation Journal* 20(4): 513–537.

Davis, J. 2000. *Threats and Promises: The Pursuit of International Influence.* Baltimore, MD: Johns Hopkins University Press.

DeRouen, K. and J. Bercovitch. 2008. "Enduring Internal Rivalries: A New Framework for the Study of Civil War." *Journal of Peace Research* 45(1): 55–74.

Diehl, P. F. 1994. *International Peacekeeping.* Revised ed. Baltimore, MD: Johns Hopkins University Press.

Diehl, P. F. 2006. "Just a Phase? Integrating Conflict Dynamics Over Time." *Conflict Management and Peace Science* 23(3): 199–210.

Diehl, P. F. and D. Druckman. 2010. *Evaluating Peace Operations.* Boulder, CO: Lynne Rienner Publishers.

Diehl, P. F. and G. Goertz. 2000. *War and Peace in International Rivalry.* Ann Arbor: University of Michigan Press.

Dixon, W. 1993. "Democracy and the Management of International Conflict." *Journal of Conflict Resolution* 37(1): 42–68.

Dixon, W. 1994. "Democracy and the Peaceful Settlement of International Conflict." *American Political Science Review* 88(1): 14–32.

Dixon, W. 1996. "Third party Techniques for Preventing Conflict Escalation and Promoting Peaceful Settlement." *International Organization* 50(4): 653–681.

Downes, A. 2004. "The Problem with Negotiated Settlements to Ethnic Civil Wars." *Security Studies* 13(4): 230–279.

Duffield, J. 2003. "Regional Conflict Management in Europe." In *Regional Conflict Management*, P. F. Diehl and J. Lepgold, eds. Lanham, MD: Rowman and Littlefield.

Eckstein, A. 2002. "Greek Mediation in the First Macedonian

War, 209–205 BC." *Historia: Zeitschrift für Alte Geschichte* 51(3): 268–297.

Eliasson, J. 2002. "Perspectives on Managing Intractable Conflict." *Negotiation Journal* 18(4): 371–374.

Ertekun, N. 1984. *The Cyprus Dispute and the Birth of the Turkish Republic of Northern Cyprus*, 2nd ed. Oxford: K. Rusten and Brother.

Falch, Å. 2009. "Towards Durable Democracy in Burundi?" Available at: www.prio.no/sptrans/-759649713/Falch (2009) Towards Durable Democracy in Burundi.pdf [Accessed May 24, 2011].

Favretto, K. 2009. "Should Peacemakers Take Sides? Major Power Mediation, Coercion and Bias." *American Political Science Review* 103(2): 248–263.

Fearon, J. 1995. "Rationalist Explanations for War." *International Organization* 49(3): 379–414.

Fearon, J. 2004. "Why Do Some Civil Wars Last So Much Longer Than Others?" *Journal of Peace Research* 41(3): 275–301.

Fisher, R. 2007. "Assessing the Contingency Model of Third Party Intervention in Successful Cases of Prenegotiation." *Journal of Peace Research* 44(3): 311–329.

Fortna, V. P. 2004. *Peace Time: Cease-Fire Agreements and the Durability of Peace*. Princeton: Princeton University Press.

Fortna, V. P. 2008. *Does Peacekeeping Work? Shaping Belligerents' Choices after Civil War*. Princeton: Princeton University Press.

Frazier, D. and W. Dixon. 2009. "Third Party Intermediaries and Negotiated Settlements, 1946–2000." In *New Approaches to Mediation*, J. Bercovitch and S. Gartner, eds. London: Routledge.

Gartner, S. and J. Bercovitch. 2006. "Overcoming Obstacles to Peace: The Contribution of Mediation to Short-Lived Settlements." *International Studies Quarterly* 50(4): 819–840.

Gartner, S. and M. Melin. 2009. "Assessing Outcomes: Conflict Management and the Durability of Peace." In *Sage Handbook of Conflict Resolution*, J. Bercovitch, V. Kremenyuk, and I. W. Zartman, eds. Los Angeles: Sage.

Gartner, S., J. Dovidio, and B. Bachman. 1996. "Revisiting the Contact Hypothesis: The Induction of a Common Ingroup Identity." *International Journal of Intercultural Relations* 20(3/4): 271–290.

Ghosn, F. 2010. "Getting to the Table and Getting to Yes: An Analysis of International Negotiations." *International Studies Quarterly* 54(4): 1055–1072.

Ghosn, F., G. Palmer, and S. Bremer. 2004. "The MID3 Data Set,

1993–2001: Procedures, Coding Rules, and Description." *Conflict Management and Peace Science* 21(2): 133–154.

Gleditsch, K. 2007. "Transnational Dimensions of Civil War." *Journal of Peace Research* 44(3): 293–309.

Goertz, G. and P. F. Diehl. 2002. "Treaties and Conflict Management in Enduring Rivalries." *International Negotiation* 7(1): 379–398.

Goertz, G., B. Jones, and P. F. Diehl. 2005. "Maintenance Processes in International Rivalries." *Journal of Conflict Resolution*, 49(5): 742–769.

Goldstein, J. and J. Pevehouse. 1997. "Reciprocity, Bullying, and International Cooperation: Time-Series Analysis of the Bosnia Conflict." *The American Political Science Review* 91(3): 515–529.

Greig, J. M. 2001. "Moments of Opportunity: Recognizing Conditions of Ripeness for International Mediation between Enduring Rivals." *Journal of Conflict Resolution* 45(6): 691–718.

Greig, J. M. 2005. "Stepping Into the Fray: When Do Mediators Mediate?" *American Journal of Political Science* 49(2): 249–266.

Greig, J. M. and P. F. Diehl. 2005. "The Peacekeeping–Peacemaking Dilemma." *International Studies Quarterly* 49(4): 621–645.

Greig, J. M. and P. F. Diehl. 2006. "Softening Up: Making Conflicts More Amenable to Diplomacy." *International Interactions* 32(4): 355–384.

Greig, J. M. and P. Regan. 2008. "When Do they Say Yes? An Analysis of the Willingness to Offer and Accept Mediation in Civil Wars." *International Studies Quarterly* 52(4): 759–781.

Grieco, J. 2001. "Repetitive Military Challenges and Recurrent International Conflicts, 1918–1994." *International Studies Quarterly* 45(2): 295–316.

Hampson, F. 2006. "The Risks of Peace: Implications for International Mediation." *Negotiation Journal* 22(1): 13–30.

Harbom, L. and P. Wallensteen. 2010. "Armed Conflicts, 1946–2009." *Journal of Peace Research* 47(4): 501–509.

Hartzell, C. and A. Yuen. 2012. "The Durability of Peace." In *Guide to the Scientific Study of International Processes*, S. M. Mitchell, P. F. Diehl, and J. Morrow, eds. London: Wiley-Blackwell.

Hensel, P. 1994. "One Thing Leads to Another: Recurrent Militarized Disputes in Latin America, 1816–1986." *Journal of Peace Research* 31(3): 281–297.

Hensel, P. and S. M. Mitchell. 2005. "Issue Indivisibility and Territorial Claims." *GeoJournal* 64 (4): 275–285.

Higgins, R. 1981. *United Nations Peacekeeping: Documents and Commentary.* Vol. IV: *Europe, 1946–1979.* New York: Oxford University Press.

Hiro, D. 1991. *The Longest War: The Iran–Iraq Military Conflict.* New York: Routledge.

Höglund, K. and I. Svensson. 2009. "Mediating between Tigers and Lions: Norwegian Peace Diplomacy in Sri Lanka's Civil War." *Contemporary South Asia* 17(2): 175–191.

Holbrooke, R. 1999. *To End a War.* New York: Random House.

Holsti, K. 1966. "Resolving International Conflicts: A Taxonomy of Behavior and Some Figures on Procedures." *Journal of Conflict Resolution* 10(3): 272–296.

Hopmann, P. T. 1996. *The Negotiation Process and the Resolution of International Conflicts.* Columbia: University of South Carolina Press.

Hume, C. 1994. *The United Nations, Iran, and Iraq.* Bloomington, IN: Indiana University Press.

Iji, T. 2001. "Multiparty Mediation in Tajikistan: The 1997 Peace Agreement." *International Negotiation* 6(3): 357–385.

Jabri, V. 1990. *Mediating Conflict: Decision-making and Western Intervention in Namibia.* New York: Manchester University Press.

Jackson, E. 1952. *Meeting of Minds: A Way to Peace through Mediation.* New York: McGraw Hill.

James, A. 1989. "The UN Force in Cyprus." *International Affairs* 89(3): 481–500.

Jervis, R. 2004. "The Implications of Prospect Theory for Human Nature and Values." *Political Psychology* 25(2): 163–176.

Johnson, R. 2011. *The Iran–Iraq War.* New York: Palgrave MacMillan.

Jones, D., S. Bremer, and J. D. Singer. 1996. "Militarized Interstate Disputes: 1816–1992: Rationale, Coding Rules, and Empirical Patterns." *Conflict Management and Peace Science* 15(2): 163–213.

Karsh, E. 2002. *The Iran–Iraq War 1980–1988.* London: Osprey.

Kaufman, S. and G. T. Duncan. 1992. "A Formal Framework for Mediator Mechanisms and Mediations." *Journal of Conflict Resolution* 36(4): 688–708.

Keesings Record of World Events. 1982.

Kelman, H. C. 1997. "Some Determinants of the Oslo Breakthrough." *International Negotiation* 2(2): 183–194.

Ker-Lindsay, J. 2000. "Greek–Turkish Rapprochement: The Impact of 'Disaster Diplomacy'?" *Cambridge Review of International Affairs* 14(1): 215–232.

Kleiboer, M. 1994. "Ripeness of Conflict: A Fruitful Notion?" *Journal of Peace Research* 31(1): 109–116.

Kleiboer, M. 1996. "Understanding Success and Failure of International Mediation." *Journal of Conflict Resolution* 40(2): 360–389.

Kochan, T. and T. Jick. 2011. "The Public Sector Mediation Process: A Theory and Empirical Examination." *Journal of Conflict Resolution* 22(2): 209–240.

Kriesberg, L. 1992. *International Conflict Resolution*. New Haven: Yale University Press.

Kriesberg, L. 2001. "Mediation and the Transformation of the Israeli–Palestinian Conflict." *Journal of Peace Research* 38(3): 373–392.

Kydd, A. 2003. "Which Side Are you On? Bias, Credibility, and Mediation." *American Journal of Political Science* 47(4): 597–611.

Kydd, A. 2006. "When Can Mediators Build Trust?" *American Political Science Review* 100(3): 449–462.

Kydd, A. and B. Walter. 2002. "Sabotaging the Peace: The Politics of Extremist Violence." *International Organization* 56(2): 263–296.

Lasensky, S. 2002. "Underwriting Peace in the Middle East: US Foreign Policy and the Limits of Economic Inducements." *Middle East Review of International Affairs* 6(1): 90–109.

Laudy, M. 2000. "The Vatican Mediation of the Beagle Channel Dispute: Crisis Intervention and Forum Building." In *Words over War: Mediation and Arbitration to Prevent Deadly Conflict*, M. Greenberg, J. Barton, and M. McGuinness, eds. Lanham: Rowman and Littlefield.

Lederach, J. 1997. *Building Peace: Sustainable Reconciliation in Divided Societies*. Washington: United States Institute of Peace Press.

Levy, J. 1997. "Prospect Theory, Rational Choice, and International Relations." *International Studies Quarterly* 41(1): 87–112.

Low, S. 1985. "The Zimbabwe Settlement, 1976–1979." In Touval and Zartman (1985b).

Luttwak, E. 2001. "The Curse of Inconclusive Intervention." In *Turbulent Peace: The Challenges of Managing International Conflict*, C. Crocker, F. Hampson, and P. Aall, eds. Washington, DC: United States Institute of Peace Press.

Maoz, I. 2005. "Evaluating the Communication between Groups in Dispute: Equality in Contact Interventions between Jews and Arabs in Israel." *Negotiation Journal* 21(1): 131–146.

Mattes, M. and B. Savun. 2009. "Fostering Peace after Civil War:

Commitment Problems and Agreement Design." *International Studies Quarterly* 53(4): 737–759.

Mattes, M. and B. Savun. 2010. "Information, Agreement Design, and the Durability of Civil War Settlements." *American Journal of Political Science* 54(2): 511–524.

Melin, M. 2011. "The Impact of State Relationships on if, when, and how Conflict Management Occurs." *International Studies Quarterly* (forthcoming).

Mitchell, C. 1995. "The Right Moment: Notes on 4 Models of Ripeness." *Paradigms* 9(2): 35–52.

Mitchell, C. 2000. *Gestures of Conciliation: Factors Contributing to Successful Olive Branches.* New York: Palgrave Macmillan.

Mitchell, S. M. 2002. "A Kantian System? Democracy and Third Party Conflict Resolution." *American Journal of Political Science* 46(4): 749–759.

Mooradian, M. and D. Druckman. 1999. "Hurting Stalemate or Mediation? The Conflict over Nagorno-Karabakh 1990–95." *Journal of Peace Research* 36(4): 709–727.

Morey, D. 2009. "Conflict and the Duration of Peace in Enduring Rivalries." *Conflict Management and Peace Science* 26(4): 331–345.

Mthembu-Salter, G. 2002. "Burundi's Peace Agreement without Peace." *Track Two* 11(5): 22–35.

Nagel, S. S. 1997. *Super-Optimum Solutions and Win-Win Policy.* Westport, CT: Greenwood Publishing.

Neack, L. and R. Knudson. 1999. "The Multiple Meanings and Purposes of Peacekeeping in Cyprus." *International Politics* 36(4): 465–502.

Ngaruko, F. and J. Nkurunziza. 2005. "Civil War and its Duration in Burundi." In *Understanding Civil War.* Vol. I: *Africa*, P. Collier and N. Sambanis, eds. Washington, DC: The World Bank.

Nilsson, D. 2008. "Partial Peace: Rebel Groups Inside and Outside of Civil War Settlements." *Journal of Peace Research* 45(4): 479–495.

Owsiak, A. 2011. "Paths to Peace: Conflict Management Trajectories in Militarized Interstate Disputes." Paper presented at the Annual Meeting of the International Studies Association, Montreal.

Paris, R. 2004. *At War's End.* Cambridge: Cambridge University Press.

Pettigrew, T. 1998. "Intergroup Contact Theory." *Annual Review of Psychology* 49: 65–85.

Pevehouse, J., T. Nordstrom, and K. Warnke. 2004. "The COW-2 International Organizations Dataset Version 2.0." *Conflict Management and Peace Science* 21(2): 101–119.

Princen, T. 1991. "Camp David: Problem-Solving or Power Politics as Usual?" *Journal of Peace Research* 28(1): 57–69.

Princen, T. 1992. *Intermediaries in International Conflict.* Princeton: Princeton University Press.

Pruitt, D. 1997. "Ripeness Theory and the Oslo Talks." *International Negotiation* 2(2): 237–250.

Pruitt, D. 2000. "The Tactics of Third Party Intervention." *Orbis* 44(2): 245–254.

Pruitt, D. 2002. "Mediator Behavior and Success in Mediation." In *Studies in International Mediation*, J. Bercovitch, ed. New York: Palgrave Macmillan.

Pruitt, D. 2005. "Whither Ripeness Theory." Institute for conflict analysis and resolution. George Mason University. Working Paper. Available at: http://gmu.edu/departments/icar/wp_25_pruitt.pdf [Accessed May 9, 2011].

Pruitt, D. 2007. "Readiness Theory and the Northern Ireland Conflict." *American Behavioral Scientist* 50(11): 1520–1541.

Pruitt, D. and J. Rubin. 1986. *Social Conflict: Escalation, Stalemate, and Settlement.* New York: Random House.

Pruitt, D., J. Bercovitch, and I. W. Zartman. 1997. "A Brief History of the Oslo Talks." *International Negotiation* 2(2): 177–182.

Quackenbush, S. L. and J. F. Venteicher. 2008. "Settlements, Outcomes, and the Recurrence of Conflict." *Journal of Peace Research* 45(6): 723–742.

Quinn, D., J. Wilkenfeld, K. Smarick, and V. Asal. 2006. "Power Play: Mediation in Symmetric and Asymmetric International Crises." *International Interactions* 32(4): 442–470.

Rauchhaus, R. 2006. "Asymmetric Information, Mediation, and Conflict Management." *World Politics* 58(2): 207–241.

Raymond, G. 1994. "Democracies, Disputes, and Third Party Intermediaries." *Journal of Conflict Resolution* 38(1): 24–42.

Regan, P. 2002. "Third Party Interventions and the Duration of Intrastate Conflict." *Journal of Conflict Resolution* 46(1): 55–73.

Regan, P. and A. Aydin. 2006. "Diplomacy and Other Forms of Intervention in Civil Wars." *Journal of Conflict Resolution* 50(5): 736–756.

Regan, P. and A. Stam. 2000. "In the Nick of Time." *International Studies Quarterly* 44(2): 239–260.

Reyntjens, F. 2005. "Briefing: Burundi: A Peaceful Transition After a Decade of War?" *African Affairs* 105(418): 117–135.

Richmond, O. 1998. "Devious Objectives and the Disputants' View of International Mediation: A Theoretical Framework." *Journal of Peace Research* 35(6): 707–722.

Richter, J. 1992. "Perpetuating the Cold War: Domestic Sources of International Patterns of Behavior." *Political Science Quarterly* 107(2): 271–302.

Rieff, D. 1995. *Slaughterhouse: Bosnia and the Failure of the West.* New York: Simon and Schuster.

Rogel, C. 2004. *The Breakup of Yugoslavia and its Aftermath.* Westport, CT: Greenwood Press.

Rothchild, D. 2002. "The Two-Phase Peace Implementation Process in Africa and its Implications for Democracy." University of Leipzig Papers on Africa, No. 59.

Rubin, J. 1992. "Conclusion: International Mediation in Context." In *Mediation in International Relations: Multiple Approaches to Conflict Management*, J. Bercovitch and J. Rubin, eds. New York: St. Martin's Press.

Sambanis, N. 1999. "The United Nations Operations in Cyprus: A New Look at the Peacekeeping–Peacemaking Relationship." *International Peacekeeping* 6(1): 79–108.

Sarkees, M. and F. Wayman. 2010. *Resort to War: 1816 – 2007.* Washington: CQ Press.

Savun, B. 2008. "Information, Bias, and Mediation Success." *International Studies Quarterly* 52(1): 25–47.

Savun, B. 2009. "Mediator Types and the Effectiveness of Information-Provision Strategies in the Resolution of International Conflict." In *New Approaches to Mediation*, J. Bercovitch and S. Gartner, eds. London: Routledge.

Schulz, H. 2004. "The Politics of Fear and the Collapse of the Mideast Peace Process." *International Journal of Peace Studies* 9(1): 85–105.

Senese, P. and J. Vasquez. 2008. *The Steps to War.* Princeton: Princeton University Press.

Shaw, C. 2003. "Conflict Management in Latin America." In *Regional Conflict Management*, P. F. Diehl and J. Lepgold, eds. Lanham, MD: Rowman and Littlefield.

Shin, S.-J. and P. F. Diehl. 2008. "Mutually Hurting Stalemate: Navigating the Conceptual Minefield." Paper presented at the Annual Meeting of the Midwest Political Science Association, Chicago.

Slantchev, B. 2004. "How Initiators End their Wars: The Duration of Warfare and the Terms of Peace." *American Journal of Political Science* 48(4): 813–829.

Smith, A. and A. Stam. 2003. "Mediation and Peacekeeping in a Random Walk Model of Civil and Interstate War." *International Studies Review* 5(4): 115–135.

Smith, W. P. 1985. "Effectiveness of the Biased Mediator." *Negotiation Journal* 1(4): 363–72.

Solomon, R. H. 1999. "Bringing Peace to Cambodia." In Crocker, Hampson, and Aall (1999).

Solomon, R. H. 2000. *Exiting Indochina: US Leadership of the Cambodia Settlement and Normalization with Vietnam.* Washington, DC: United States Institute of Peace Press.

Souresrafil, B. 1989. *The Iran–Iraq War.* Plainview, NY: Guinan, Co.

Spector, B. 1998. "Deciding to Negotiate with Villains." *Negotiation Journal* 14(1): 43–60.

Sremac, D. 1999. *War of Words.* Westport, CT: Praeger.

Stedman, S. 1997. "Spoiler Problems in Peace Processes." *International Security* 22(2): 5–53.

Stein, J. G. 1989. "Getting to the Table: The Triggers, Stages, Functions, and Consequences of Prenegotiation." In *Getting to the Table,* J. G. Stein, ed. Baltimore: Johns Hopkins University Press.

Stein, J. 1996. "Image Identity and Conflict Resolution." In *Managing Global Chaos: Sources of and Responses to International Conflict,* C. Crocker, F. Hampson, and P. Aall, eds. Washington: United States Institute of Peace Press.

Stein, K. and S. Lewis. 1996. "Mediation in the Middle East." In *Managing Global Chaos: Sources of and Responses to International Conflict,* C. Crocker, F. Hampson, and P. Aall, eds. Washington: United States Institute of Peace Press.

Svensson, I. 2007a. "Mediation with Muscles or Minds? Exploring Power Mediators and Pure Mediators in Civil Wars." *International Negotiation* 12(2): 229–248.

Svensson, I. 2007b. "Bargaining, Bias and Peace Brokers: How Rebels Commit to Peace." *Journal of Peace Research* 44(2): 177–194.

Svensson, I. 2007c. "Fighting with Faith." *Journal of Conflict Resolution* 51(6): 930–949.

Toft, M. 2010. "Ending Civil Wars: A Case for Rebel Victory?" *International Security* 34(4): 7–36.

Touval, S. 1975. "Biased Intermediaries: Theoretical and Historical

Considerations." *Jerusalem Journal of International Relations* 1(1): 51–69.

Touval, S. 1982. *The Peace Brokers: Mediators in the Arab–Israeli Conflict 1948–1979*. Princeton: Princeton University Press.

Touval, S. 1992. "The Superpowers as Mediators." In *Mediation in International Relations: Multiple Approaches to Conflict Management*, J. Bercovitch and J. Rubin, eds. New York: St. Martin's Press.

Touval, S. 2000. "The Impact of Multiple Asymmetries on Israeli–Palestinian Negotiations." In *Power and Negotiation*, I. W. Zartman and J. Z. Rubin, eds. Ann Arbor: University of Michigan Press.

Touval, S. 2003. "Mediation and Foreign Policy." *International Studies Review* 5(4): 91–95.

Touval, S. and I. W. Zartman. 1985a. "Mediation in Theory." In Touval and Zartman (1985b).

Touval, S. and I. W. Zartman, eds. 1985b. *International Mediation in Theory and Practice*. Boulder, CO: Westview Press.

Turay, T. 2000. "Civil Society and Peacebuilding: The Role of the Inter-Religious Council of Sierra Leone." *Paying the Price: Sierra Leone's Peace Process*. Available at: ACCORD Conciliation Resource. http://www.c-r.org/our-work/accord/ sierra-leone/inter-religious-council. php [Accessed July 21, 2011].

Vervaeke, Koen. 2003. "Peace, Mediation and Reconciliation: The Belgian experience." Belgian–Norwegian Seminar on Peace, Mediation and Reconciliation – Brussels. Available at: http://www.egmontinstitute.be/speechnotes/02-03/030521-Vervaeke%20Norv-Be.pdf [Accessed May 1, 2011].

Wagner, R. 2000. "Bargaining and War." *American Journal of Political Science* 44(3): 469–484.

Wall, J., J. Stark, and R. Standifer. 2001. "Mediation – A Current Review and Theory Development." *Journal of Conflict Resolution* 45(3): 370–391.

Walter, B. F. 1997. "The Critical Barrier to Civil War Settlement." *International Organization* 51(3): 335–364.

Walter, B. F. 2002. *Committing to Peace: The Successful Settlement of Civil Wars*. Princeton: Princeton University Press.

Weiss, T. G. 2007. *Humanitarian Intervention: Ideas in Action*. Cambridge: Polity Press.

Wennmann, A. (2009). "Getting Armed Groups to the Table: Peace Processes, the Political Economy of Conflict and the Mediated State." *Third World Quarterly* 30(6): 1123–1138.

Wilkenfeld, J., K. Young, V. Asal, and D. Quinn. 2003. "Mediating International Crises: Cross-National and Experimental Perspectives." *Journal of Conflict Resolution* 47(3): 279–301.

Young, O. 1967. *The Intermediaries: Third Parties in International Crises.* Princeton: Princeton University Press.

Zartman, I. W. 1981. "Explaining Disengagement." In *Dynamics of Third Party Intervention: Kissinger in the Middle East,* J. Rubin, ed. New York: Praeger.

Zartman, I. W. 1989. *Ripe for Resolution: Conflict and Intervention in Africa.* New York: Oxford University Press.

Zartman, I. W. 1991. "Conflict and Resolution: Contest, Cost, and Change." *The ANNALS of the American Academy of Political and Social Science* 518(1): 11–22.

Zartman, I. W. 2000. "Ripeness: The Hurting Stalemate and Beyond". In *International Conflict Resolution after the Cold War,* P. Stern and D. Druckman, eds. Washington: National Academy Press.

Zartman, I. W. 2001. "The Timing of Peace Initiatives: Hurting Stalemates and Ripe Moments." *Ethnopolitics* 1(1): 8–18.

Zartman, I. W. 2002. "Mediation by Regional Organizations: the OAU in Chad and Congo." In *Studies in International Mediaton,* J. Bercovitch, ed. New York: Palgrave MacMillan.

Zartman, I. W. 2003. "Ripeness." The Beyond Intractability Knowledge Base Project. Available at: http://www.beyondintractability.org/essay/ripeness/?nid=1029 [Accessed July 21, 2011].

Zartman, I. W. 2007a. "The Timing of Peace Initiatives: Hurting Stalemates and Ripe Moments." In *Contemporary Peacemaking: Conflict, Violence and Peace Processes,* 2nd ed., J. Darby and R. MacGinty, eds. New York: Palgrave Macmillan.

Zartman, I. W. 2007b. "Ripeness Revisited: The Push and Pull of Conflict Management." In *Deeskalation von Gewaltkonflikten seit 1945,* Corinna Hauswedell, ed. Essen: Klartext-Verlagsges.

Zartman, I. W. 2008. *Negotiation and Conflict Management.* New York: Routledge.

Zartman, I. W. and S. Touval. 1985. "International Mediation: Conflict Resolution and Power Politics." *Journal of Social Issues* 41(2): 27–45.

Zubek, J., D. Pruitt, R. Peirce, N. McGillicuddy, and H. Syna. 1992. "Disputant and Mediator Behaviors Affecting Short-Term Success in Mediation." *Journal of Conflict Resolution* 36(3): 546–572.

Index